70 SALSAS, DIPS & DRESSINGS

70 SALSAS, DIPS & DRESSINGS

FABULOUS AND EASY-TO-MAKE ACCOMPANIMENTS TO TRANSFORM
YOUR COOKING, SHOWN STEP BY STEP IN OVER 340 PHOTOGRAPHS

CHRISTINE FRANCE

southwater

Acknowledgements

Thanks to the following photographers: Karl Adamson, Edward Allwright, David Armstrong, Steve Baxter, James Duncan, John Freeman, Michelle Garrett, John Heseltine, Amanda Heywood, Janine Hosegood, Don Last, Michael Michaels, Patrick McLeavy, Thomas Odulate, Debbie Patterson, Juliet Piddington and William Lingwood.

Recipes by: Alex Barker, Angela Boggiano, Carla Capalbo, Jacqueline Clark, Carole Clements, Roz Denny, Nicola Diggins, Tessa Evelegh, Joanna Farrow, Christine France, Silvana Franco, Shirley Gill, Nicola Graimes, Juliet Harbutt, Christine Ingram, Peter Jordan, Soheila Kimberley, Ruby Le Bois, Lesley Macklay, Sue Maggs, Maggie Mayhew, Sallie Morris, Janice Murfitt, Maggie Pannell, Louise Pickford, Katherine Richmond, Laura Washburn, Steven Wheeler, Kate Whiteman and Jeni Wright.

This edition is published by Southwater, an imprint of Anness Publishing Ltd, Hermes House, 88–89 Blackfriars Road, London SE1 8HA;
tel. 020 7401 2077; fax 020 7633 9499

www.southwaterbooks.com; www.annesspublishing.com

If you like the images in this book and would like to investigate using them for publishing, promotions or advertising, please visit our website www.practicalpictures.com for more information.

UK agent: The Manning Partnership Ltd;
tel. 01225 478444; fax 01225 478440; sales@manning-partnership.co.uk
UK distributor: Grantham Book Services Ltd;
tel. 01476 541080; fax 01476 541061; orders@gbs.tbs-ltd.co.uk
North American agent/distributor: National Book Network;
tel. 301 459 3366; fax 301 429 5746; www.nbnbooks.com
Australian agent/distributor: Pan Macmillan Australia;
tel. 1300 135 113; fax 1300 135 103; customer.service@macmillan.com.au
New Zealand agent/distributor: David Bateman Ltd;
tel. (09) 415 7664; fax (09) 415 8892

Publisher: Joanna Lorenz
Managing Editor: Judith Simons
Project Editor: Simona Hill
Designer: Simon Wilder
Editorial Reader: Richard McGinlay
Production Controller: Claire Rae

ETHICAL TRADING POLICY
Because of our ongoing ecological investment programme, you, as our customer, can have the pleasure and reassurance of knowing that a tree is being cultivated on your behalf to naturally replace the materials used to make the book you are holding. For further information about this scheme, go to www.annesspublishing.com/trees

A CIP catalogue record for this book is available from the British Library.

Previously published as *Salsas, Dips, Dressings and Marinades*

Main front cover image shows Guacamole – for recipe, see page 42.

NOTES
Bracketed terms are intended for American readers.

For all recipes, quantities are given in both metric and imperial measures and, where appropriate, in standard cups and spoons. Follow one set of measures, but not a mixture, because they are not interchangeable.

Standard spoon and cup measures are level. 1 tsp = 5ml, 1 tbsp = 15ml, 1 cup = 250ml/8fl oz.

Australian standard tablespoons are 20ml. Australian readers should use 3 tsp in place of 1 tbsp for measuring small quantities. American pints are 16fl oz/2 cups. American readers should use 20fl oz/2.5 cups in place of 1 pint when measuring liquids.

Electric oven temperatures in this book are for conventional ovens. When using a fan oven, the temperature will probably need to be reduced by about 10–20°C/20–40°F. Since ovens vary, you should check with your manufacturer's instruction book for guidance.

Medium (US large) eggs are used unless otherwise stated.

Contents

Introduction

If salsas, dressings and marinades evoke images of warm summer weather, easy outdoor living and *al fresco* dining, then this collection of superb, flavour-packed recipes is sure to set your taste-buds tingling. Using tasty, fresh ingredients, bursting with vitality, salsas and dips are quick to prepare, fun to make and are a guaranteed easy-entertaining menu option. Colourful and crunchy, spicy and aromatic or smooth and creamy, here are simple, no-cook recipes for sweet and savoury dishes for every time of day.

Enliven a simple dish, such as grilled fish, baked potatoes or a basic salad with tempting and tangy mixtures of fruits, vegetables, herbs, oils and spices. Whatever main dish you are serving, there will be a suitable succulent salsa or delectable dip to add piquancy, freshness, richness or fiery heat.

Like salsas and dips, marinades and dressings can be prepared in advance and kept in the refrigerator until they are needed. These no-fuss recipes are ideal for fish, meat and poultry dishes, not only enhancing the flavour, but also often tenderizing as well. Simply whisk together the ingredients in a bowl or shake them together in a screw-top jar.

Make the most of the summer and autumn abundance of fruit with this wonderful collection of recipes for chutneys and relishes. Mellow and comforting, sharp and spicy or fresh and fruity, home-made relishes add depth and contrast to cold meats, cheese and summer salads.

Whatever your taste and whatever the occasion, there are recipes here to add fun and sparkle to all your meals – from a barbecue party to Sunday brunch and pre-dinner drinks.

Fresh Fruit

Salsas made with fresh fruit are among the most popular, and fruit is one of the most essential ingredients in home-made chutneys. The recipes which follow make exciting use of a wide variety of fruits, whether old favourites, such as apples and oranges, or exotic and tropical imports, such as mangoes and papaya. Different fruits may be used together to make a refreshing, summery salsa, mixed with yogurt and herbs for a creamy dip or spiced with chillies, onions and ginger to fire up the party.

APPLES

These orchard fruits are available in thousands of varieties, although the choice available in super-markets is often restricted to only a few. Organic fruit is thought to have the best flavour and it is worth choosing apples with attractive coloured skins for any recipes where the apples are to be left unpeeled. For sweetness, use eating apples for making uncooked relishes, but for cooked relishes such as chutneys use cooking apples. When buying apples, choose bright, firm fruits without any bruises. Store in a cool place away from direct sunlight.

NECTARINES AND PEACHES

These summer fruits are prized for their perfume and sweet juicy flesh. Nectarines are like peaches without the fuzzy skin, but have a similar flavour. Both are used in salsas. These fruits bruise easily, so buy them slightly underripe. To ripen them, place in a brown paper bag with an already ripened fruit.

Above: Cooking and eating apples

Removing the Stone or Pit from Fruit

1 To remove the stone (pit) from peaches, nectarines, apricots or plums, cut around the middle of the fruit down to the stone. Twist each half of the fruit in opposite directions.

2 Prise out the stone using the tip of the knife and discard. Rub the cut flesh with lemon juice.

Above: Mangoes

MANGOES

Mango is just one of many exotic juicy and fleshy fruits that are wonderful for serving fresh in salsas and dips, or cooking into sweet chutney. The ripeness of mango is not determined by colour, and the fruits can vary from green to yellow, orange and red in colour, although an entirely green fruit is unripe.

Preparing Mangoes

Mangoes can be fiddly to prepare because they have a large, flat stone (pit) that is slightly off-centre. The method below produces cubed fruit. Alternatively, the mango can be peeled with a vegetable peeler and sliced around the central stone.

1 Hold the fruit with one hand and cut vertically down one side of the stone. Repeat on the opposite side. Pull the flesh away from the stone. Cut any remaining flesh from the stone.

2 Taking the two large slices, and using a sharp knife, cut the flesh into a criss-cross pattern down to the skin. Holding the mango skin-side down, press it inside out, then cut the mango cubes away from the skin.

BANANAS

Creamy in texture and full of flavour, bananas almost qualify as a convenience food as they are so simple to prepare and full of nourishment. Although most popular as ingredients for dessert dips, they can be combined with savoury flavours. Their close relative, the plantain, is also a good choice for salsas, but must always be cooked first.

MELONS

Supermarkets now stock a wide variety of melons throughout the year. Crisp-fleshed watermelons are wonderfully refreshing and make a colourful addition to a fruity salsa. Orange-fleshed varieties, such as Charentais and Canteloupe, are also particularly attractive and their sweetness provides an intriguing contrast with ingredients, such as onions and herbs, in savoury salsas.

ORANGES

Citrus fruits are best known for their high vitamin C content, and their sweet, slightly acid flavour. Oranges are invaluable for dressings and fruit salsas, and their zest is used as a flavouring in relishes and chutneys. Use within two weeks of purchase.

LEMONS AND LIMES

The juice and rind of lemons and limes are essential for many dressings, marinades and relishes. They are virtually interchangeable, although limes tend to be sourer than lemons. All citrus fruit releases more juice if squeezed at room temperature.

Right: Oranges

Below: Bananas

PAPAYA

Also known as pawpaw, the papaya is a sweet-fleshed fruit with numerous edible small black seeds, which are quite peppery. Unripe papaya is excellent in marinades because it contains a tenderizing enzyme, but fruit for uncooked salsas and dips should always be ripe.

Above: Papaya

PINEAPPLES

These tropical fruits are distinctive looking, with spiky green leaves. The flesh is sweet and juicy. Pineapple can be used in sweet and savoury dishes but must be served when ripe. Choose fruit that feels firm with a definite pineapple aroma; a leaf pulled from the centre should come away easily. To prepare, cut off the leafy top and the base with a strong knife, then carve the skin from the sides.

Grating Citrus Rind

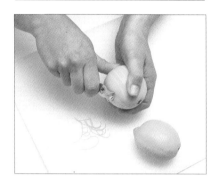

To remove long, thin shreds of rind, use a zester. Scrape it along the surface of the fruit, applying firm pressure. For finer shreds, use a grater. Rub the fruit over the fine cutters to remove the rind without any of the white pith.

Cutting Fine Strips

Using a vegetable peeler, remove strips of rind, making sure the white pith is left behind on the fruit.

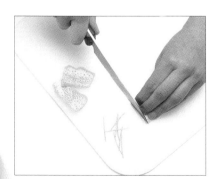

2 Stack strips of rind and, using a sharp knife, cut into fine strips.

Fresh Vegetables

As many salsas are based on vegetables as they are on fruit. Tomatoes and bell peppers, with their sweet flavours are often combined with fruit. These versatile vegetables may be used raw, blanched, cooked and, in some instances, chargrilled. In addition, raw vegetables make a delicious snack when served with a creamy dip.

Below: Aubergines (Eggplant)

AUBERGINES

The dark purple, glossy-skinned aubergine (eggplant) is the most familiar variety, although it was the small ivory variety that inspired the alternative and descriptive name of eggplant. Aubergines are delicious roasted or griddled and then puréed to make a creamy dip.

CHILLIES

Known for their hot fiery taste, chillies range in potency from mild and flavourful to blisteringly hot. There are more than 200 different types of chilli, ranging from long and narrow anaheim to the lantern-shaped habanero.

TOMATOES

There are dozens of varieties of tomatoes to choose from, in a range of sizes, shapes and colours. Look for deep red fruit with a firm, yielding flesh.

Above: Chillies

Right: Tomatoes

Preparing chillies

Handle chillies with care as they can irritate the skin and eyes. It is advisable to wear gloves when preparing chillies.

The heat in chillies is contained largely in the seeds, so for a less hot dish, split the pod lengthways and remove the seeds with a knife. Smaller chillies contain more seeds than large chillies.

Peeling Tomatoes

1 Immerse the tomatoes in boiling water and leave for about 30 seconds – the base of each tomato can be slashed to make peeling easier. Alternatively, skewer each tomato on a fork, and hold over a gas flame until the skin wrinkles.

2 Lift out the tomatoes with a slotted spoon, plunge into cold water to cool slightly, and peel off the skin. Cut the tomatoes in half, then scoop out the seeds and remove the hard core. Dice or roughly chop the flesh according to the recipe.

Below: Avocados

AVOCADOS

Avocados are usually eaten raw. Slices and chunks of the peeled flesh are delicious in salads. In Mexico, where they grow in abundance, there are countless dishes based on avocados, of which guacamole is by far the best known.

PUMPKINS AND OTHER SQUASH

Available in a variety of shapes and sizes, pumpkins are deep orange in colour. Smaller pumpkins have sweeter less fibrous flesh than large ones. Other popular squashes include butternut and pattypan. All need peeling and cooking and are especially delicious when roasted.

Above: Pumpkins

PEPPERS

Sweet in taste and with a refreshing juicy flesh, (bell) peppers have a crisp texture when eaten raw. They range in colour from green to orange, yellow, red and even purple. Roasting or chargrilling the peppers enhances their sweetness.

Roasting Vegetables

Many puréed sauces or salsas call for cooked or chargrilled vegetables. Chargrilling on a barbecue is the best way to get the finest flavour from many vegetables, such as peppers, aubergines, tomatoes, garlic or onions. Barbecues retain and caramelize the flavourful juices and tenderize the flesh. However, since this method is not always practical, the next best option is to roast the vegetables on a baking sheet under a grill (broiler).

1 Cut the vegetables in half, leaving the skins on, and, if necessary, remove any seeds and cores. Place the vegetables cut-side down on a baking sheet. Place under a very hot grill, or in a hot oven, and cook until the skins are blackened and charred, and the flesh is tender.

Right: Various bell peppers

2 Remove the vegetables from the heat and set aside until they are cool enough to handle. Carefully peel off the skins from the peppers and the onions. Alternatively, put the hot bell peppers in a plastic bag and leave until they cool – the steam will encourage the skin to peel away easily.

3 Peel off the skin, then slice or chop the flesh according to the recipe. Peppers may also be roasted whole, then when cool, peel off the skin and cut them in half. Remove the core and seeds, before slicing or chopping.

Pantry Ingredients

No salsa, marinade, relish or dip would be complete without the addition of at least one culinary herb or aromatic spice – whether it is a subtle combination of mellow herbs finely chopped and added just before serving or a fragrant blend of roasted spices combined with a soy marinade. Fine, naturally full-bodied oils and flavoured oils and vinegars have an important place too, providing depth to dressings and marinades.

Below, clockwise from top left: Coriander (cilantro), parsley, chives

CULINARY HERBS

While dried herbs are useful for emergencies, always plump for fresh ones if possible, and use on the day of purchase. Otherwise store them in a plastic bag with the stems in a container of water, in the refrigerator. Store dried herbs in airtight containers in a cool, dark, dry place. When using herbs, treat the measures given in recipes as a general guide and add the herbs according to preference.

SPICES

Keep a store of spices in airtight containers in a dry, dark place in the kitchen. Buy spices in small quantities as they quickly lose their pungency.

Cinnamon sticks: These have a warm, sweet flavour and are widely used in sweet sauces and chutneys.

Coriander: The seeds are used in chutneys and have a mild sweet flavour.

Cumin: A key ingredient in chutneys and in curries, these seeds have a strong and slightly bitter taste.

Curry paste: This is sold in a range of strengths and flavours.

Chilli powder and dried chillies: Useful for adding a touch of heat to salsas and chutneys, these are usually very fiery and should be handled with caution. Some brands of chilli powder incorporate other ingredients, so always check the labels before using.

Whole nutmeg: Freshly grated whole nutmeg is much better than the powdered variety which quickly loses its flavour.

SALT AND PEPPER

Keep a supply of good-quality sea salt. It is more expensive than other types of salt, but has a more intense flavour.

Black, white and green peppercorns are all worth storing. Black peppercorns have a strong, hot flavour. White peppercorns are milder and are often preferred for light-coloured sauces.

Below, clockwise from bowl: Tandoori curry paste, nutmeg, cinnamon sticks, vanilla pods, salt, whole coriander seeds, cumin seeds, black, green and white peppercorns

OILS

These are fats that are liquid at room temperature and are used in emulsion sauces, such as mayonnaise, or in salad dressings, usually balanced with vinegar or other acids, such as lemon juice. The choice of individual oils for a particular salsa or marinade depends largely on flavour and personal taste.

Groundnut (peanut) oil: This has a mild flavour that goes well with most ingredients.

Sesame seed oil: Usually used for flavouring Asian dishes, it has an intense rich flavour.

Soya oil: A mild-flavoured oil, soya keeps well and is economical to use.

Sunflower oil: This is a versatile, light-flavoured oil that is good for sauces and dressings.

Nut oils: Walnut and hazelnut are the most commonly used nut oils for dressings, lending their rich, distinctive flavours to salads.

Olive oil: The characteristics of olive oils vary and depend on variety, growing region and method of production. For most sauces, including mayonnaise, virgin olive oil is usually the best choice. Extra virgin olive oil, from the first cold pressing, has a very distinctive flavour and pungent aroma. It is expensive, but delicious in salad dressings. Pure olive oil is usually blended and may have been heat-treated. It is best reserved for cooking.

VINEGARS

Made from wine or cider, vinegars vary in strength and flavour. They are useful for salad dressings, providing a sharp, acidic contrast to the oil. The sweet-sour flavour of balsamic vinegar is best for salsas and dips.

SAUCES

A range of ready-made sauces makes preparing salsas and dips quick work.

Hoisin sauce: This sweet, thick, Chinese sauce has a rich flavour, and goes well with Asian ingredients and flavourings. It has an affinity with tomatoes.

Horseradish sauce and creamed horseradish: This adds a peppery flavour to creamy sauces.

Soy sauce: Made from fermented soya beans, this classic Chinese sauce adds a salty, sweet, rich flavour.

Tabasco sauce: Made from hot chillies. Use Tabasco sparingly to pep up salsas and marinades. The original sauce was made from red chillies.

Worcestershire sauce: A full-bodied, savoury sauce, Worcestershire sauce is made to a secret recipe, which includes garlic, shallots, chillies, anchovies and malt vinegar.

MUSTARDS

There are many varieties of mustard all of which are useful for whisking into dressings, dips and sauces. Whole grain mustard has a mild flavour and a good texture and it tastes great stirred into Greek-style (US strained plain) yogurt and mayonnaise.

Below, from left: Groundnut oil, sunflower oil, soya oil, sesame oil and walnut oil

Making Marinades and Dressings

Marinades can be savoury, sweet, spicy, fruity, fragrant or exotic, to add a contrasting flavour to all kinds of foods. They're useful not only for adding flavour, but also for tenderizing and keeping foods moist during cooking, and can also be used to form the basis of a sauce to serve with the finished dish.

Oil-based Marinades

Choose an oil-based marinade for low-fat foods, such as lean meat, poultry or white fish, which may dry out during cooking. Oil-based marinades are especially useful for basting the meat or fish before grilling (broiling) and barbecuing, and at their simplest consist of oil with crushed garlic and chopped herbs. Add crushed chillies for a hot and spicy marinade. Avoid adding salt to a marinade as this draws the juices out of the meat.

1 Place the marinade ingredients in a measuring jug (cup) and beat well with a fork to mix thoroughly. Arrange the food in a single layer in a non-metallic dish and pour the marinade over.

2 Turn the food to coat evenly in the marinade. Cover and leave in the refrigerator to marinate for 30 minutes to several hours, depending on the recipe. Turn the food occasionally.

3 When ready to cook, remove the food from the marinade. The marinade can be poured into a small pan and simmered for several minutes until thoroughly heated, then served spooned over the cooked food.

Wine- or Vinegar-based Marinades

Wine- or vinegar-based mixtures are best with rich foods such as game or oily fish, to add flavour, and to contrast and balance richness. Use herb-flavoured vinegars for oily fish and add chopped fresh herbs, such as tarragon, parsley, coriander (cilantro) and thyme.

The acid in the wine or vinegar starts the tenderizing process well before cooking. For game, which can have a tendency to be tough, leave in the marinade overnight. Add lemon juice, garlic, black pepper and herbs, and even sherry, cider or orange juice according to your preference.

Yogurt is a good marinade and can be flavoured with crushed garlic, lemon juice, and handfuls of chopped mint, thyme or rosemary for grilled lamb or pork. For fish or shellfish, use a marinade based on lemon juice with a little oil and plenty of black pepper.

1 Measure the ingredients into a jug or cup and beat with a fork to combine.

2 Arrange the food in a wide, non-metallic dish in a single layer and spoon over the marinade, turning the food to coat evenly. Cover with clear film and chill for 30 minutes up to several hours, depending on the recipe.

3 Drain the food of excess marinade before cooking. If the food is to be griddled or grilled, use the marinade to brush over the food during cooking to add extra flavour and keep it moist.

Making an Oil-based Dressing

A good vinaigrette can do more than dress a salad. It can also be used to baste meat, poultry, shellfish or vegetables during cooking. Many classic dressings, such as vinaigrette or French dressing, are based on an oil and acid mixture. The basic proportions are 3 parts oil to 1 part acid beaten together to form an emulsion. This can be done by simply whisking with a fork in a bowl, or the ingredients can be placed in a screw-top jar and shaken thoroughly. The oil you choose for a dressing adds character to the flavour, and which one you use for which dressing depends upon your own taste and upon the salad ingredients. A strongly flavoured extra virgin olive oil adds personality to a simple green leaf or potato salad, but can overpower more delicate ingredients. Pure olive oil or sunflower oil adds a lighter flavour. Nut oils, such as walnut or hazelnut, are expensive, but can add a distinctive unusual flavour to a salad when used in small quantities.

The acid in a dressing may be vinegar or lemon juice, and this can define

VARIATIONS

- *Use red or white wine vinegar, or use a herb-flavoured vinegar.*
- *Use lemon juice instead of vinegar.*
- *Replace 1 tablespoon of the vinegar with wine.*
- *Use olive oil, or a mixture of vegetable and olive oils.*
- *Use 4fl oz/120ml olive oil and 30ml/2 tbsp walnut or hazelnut oil.*
- *Add 15–30ml/1–2 tbsp Dijon mustard to the vinegar before whisking in the oil.*
- *Add 1 crushed garlic clove before whisking in the oil.*
- *Add 15–30ml/1–2 tbsp chopped herbs (parsley, basil, chives, thyme, etc) to the vinaigrette.*

the flavour of the finished salad. Choose from wine, sherry or cider vinegars, herb, chilli or fruit vinegars, to balance or contrast with the salad ingredients and the type of oil. Matured vinegars such as balsamic can be strong in flavour. Balsamic has a distinctive flavour, because of its aging in wooden barrels and so the basic proportions of 3 parts oil to 1 of vinegar should be amended to 5 parts oil and 2 of balsamic vinegar. Lemon juice adds a sharper flavour, which can be useful to add a lively tang to a bland dish. Other fruit juices, such as orange or apple juice can be used instead for a sweeter, less acid flavour.

Classic Vinaigrette

To ensure the ingredients blend together in a smooth emulsion, make sure that all the ingredients are at room temperature.

Put 30ml/2 tbsp vinegar in a bowl with 10ml/2 tsp Dijon mustard, salt and ground black pepper. Add 1.5ml/¼ tsp caster (superfine) sugar if you like. Whisk to combine.

Slowly drizzle in 90ml/6 tbsp oil, whisking constantly, until the vinaigrette is smooth and well blended. Check the seasoning and adjust if necessary.

Creamy Orange Dressing

This tangy orange dressing is versatile enough to complement a mixed green salad with orange segments and tomatoes. It could also partner grilled chicken or smoked duck breasts, or chicken kebabs, served on a bed of rice salad.

Serves 4

45ml/3 tbsp half-fat crème fraîche
15ml/1 tbsp white wine vinegar
*finely grated rind and juice of
    1 small orange*
salt and ground black pepper

1 Measure the crème fraîche and wine vinegar into a screw-top jar with the orange rind and juice.

2 Shake well until evenly combined, then adjust the seasoning to taste as desired.

Salsas

"Salsa" is simply translated as "sauce", but since the sauces we refer to as salsas originated in the rich, colourful tradition of Mexican cooking, they have a very different style from the familiar types of classic sauces of other cuisines. They're perfect for summer eating, and an ideal choice to accompany barbecued (grilled) or grilled (broiled) foods.

Fresh, colourful chillies are finely chopped and tossed imaginatively with fruits, vegetables or herbs to create highly individual combinations that enliven any dish or simple meal, from fish to meat, and from vegetables to eggs. Salsas may be fiery-hot, or delicately spiced, or sweet and sour, or just hot and sweet – depending on your taste and the food it will accompany.

The most basic salsas are "crudo", which simply means raw, so the ingredients take no more preparation than fine chopping or processing in a blender to combine. The most typical Mexican salsa crudo would have chillies, onions, tomatoes or bell peppers with fresh coriander (cilantro), for a simple, vibrant, zesty mix. Others can be more elaborate, sometimes simmered to soften ingredients and mingle flavours, or with the addition of exotic fruits or spices. Above all, salsas are an opportunity to show off your creative flair – try some of our varied recipes, then start experimenting with your own.

Salsa Verde

THERE ARE MANY VERSIONS of this classic green salsa. Try this one drizzled over chargrilled squid, or with baked potatoes served with a green salad.

Serves 4

INGREDIENTS

2–4 green chillies, halved
8 spring onions (scallions)
2 garlic cloves
50g/2oz salted capers
sprig of fresh tarragon
bunch of fresh parsley
grated rind and juice of 1 lime
juice of 1 lemon
90ml/6 tbsp olive oil
about 15ml/1 tbsp green Tabasco sauce
ground black pepper

2 Use your fingers to rub the excess salt off the capers. Add them, with the tarragon and parsley, to the food processor and pulse again until the ingredients are quite finely chopped.

3 Transfer the mixture to a bowl. Mix in the lime rind and juice, lemon juice and olive oil, stirring lightly so the citrus juice and oil do not emulsify.

1 Halve and seed the chillies and trim the spring onions. Halve the garlic cloves. Place in a food processor and pulse briefly.

COOK'S TIP

Some salted capers are quite strong and may need rinsing before use. If you prefer, you may use pickled capers instead.

4 Add green Tabasco sauce, a little at a time, and black pepper to taste.

5 Cover and chill the salsa in the refrigerator until ready to serve, but do not prepare it more than 8 hours in advance.

Coriander Pesto Salsa

THIS AROMATIC SALSA IS delicious drizzled over fish and chicken, tossed with pasta ribbons or used to dress a fresh avocado and tomato salad. To transform it into a dip, simply mix with a little mayonnaise or sour cream.

Serves 4

INGREDIENTS

50g/2oz fresh coriander (cilantro) leaves
15g/½oz fresh parsley
2 red chillies
1 garlic clove
50g/2oz/⅓ cup shelled pistachio nuts
25g/1oz/⅓ cup finely grated Parmesan cheese, plus extra to garnish
90ml/6 tbsp olive oil
juice of 2 limes
salt and ground black pepper

3 Add the pistachio nuts to the herb mixture and pulse the power until they are roughly chopped. Stir in the Parmesan cheese, olive oil and lime juice.

4 Add salt and pepper to taste. Spoon the mixture into a serving bowl and cover and chill until ready to serve, garnished with Parmesan.

VARIATION

Any number of different herbs or nuts may be used to make a similar salsa to this one – try a mixture of rosemary and parsley, or add a handful of black olives.

1 Process the fresh coriander and parsley in a food processor or blender until finely chopped.

2 Halve the chillies lengthways and remove their seeds. Add to the herbs together with the garlic, and process until finely chopped.

Double Chilli Salsa

THIS IS A SCORCHINGLY hot salsa for only the very brave! Spread it sparingly on to cooked meats and burgers for a real kick.

Serves 4–6

INGREDIENTS

6 habanero chillies or Scotch bonnets
2 ripe tomatoes
4 standard green jalapeño chillies
30ml/2 tbsp chopped fresh parsley
30ml/2 tbsp olive oil
15ml/1 tbsp balsamic or sherry vinegar
salt

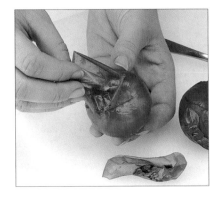

1 Skewer a habanero or Scotch bonnet chilli on to a metal fork and hold it in a gas flame for 2–3 minutes, turning the chilli until the skin blackens and blisters. Repeat with all the habaneros or Scotch bonnets, then set aside until cool.

2 Skewer the tomatoes, one at a time, and hold them in the gas flame for 1–2 minutes, or until the skin wrinkles. Slip off the skins and halve. Use a teaspoon to scoop out and discard the seeds. Finely chop the flesh.

3 Rub the skins off the cooled chillies with a clean dishtowel. Do not touch the chillies with your hands: use a fork to hold them and slice them open with a sharp knife. Scrape out and discard the seeds, then finely chop the flesh.

4 Halve the jalapeño chillies, remove their seeds and finely slice them widthways into tiny strips.

5 Mix together both types of chilli, the tomatoes and chopped parsley.

6 Mix the olive oil, vinegar and a little salt, pour this over the salsa and cover the dish. Chill for up to 3 days.

VARIATION

Habanero chillies and Scotch bonnets are among the hottest fresh chillies available. You may prefer to tone down the heat of this salsa by using a milder variety.

Tomato Salsa

THIS SIMPLE SIDE DISH is very versatile and really enhances a wide range of hot and cold dishes.

Serves 6

INGREDIENTS

6 medium tomatoes
1 green Kenyan chilli
2 spring onions (scallions), chopped
10cm/4in length cucumber, diced
30ml/2 tbsp lemon juice
30ml/2 tbsp chopped fresh
    coriander (cilantro)
15ml/1 tbsp fresh parsley, chopped
salt and ground black pepper

1 Cut a small cross in the stalk end of each tomato. Place in a bowl and cover with boiling water.

2 After 30 seconds or as soon as the skins split, drain and plunge into cold water. Gently slide off the skins. Quarter the tomatoes, remove the seeds and dice the flesh.

3 Halve the chilli, remove the stalk, seeds and the membrane, and chop the flesh finely.

4 Mix together all the ingredients and transfer to a serving bowl. Chill for 1–2 hours before serving.

VARIATIONS

To make Tomato and Caper Salsa
Prepare the tomatoes and stir in the onion and lemon juice. Add 6 torn sprigs of basil and 15ml/1 tbsp roughly chopped capers. Season to taste.

To make Tomato and (Bell) Pepper Salsa
Prepare 4 tomatoes and stir in the chilli, onion and herbs. Add a roasted, peeled and diced orange pepper and a crushed garlic clove. Season to taste.

Chilli and Coconut Salsa

A SWEET-AND-SOUR SALSA, spiked with chillies, that goes well with grilled or barbecued fish.

Serves 6–8

INGREDIENTS

1 small coconut
1 small pineapple
2 green Kenyan chillies
5cm/2in piece lemon grass
60ml/4 tbsp natural (plain) yogurt
2.5ml/½ tsp salt
30ml/2 tbsp chopped fresh
   coriander (cilantro)
fresh coriander (cilantro) sprigs, to garnish

1 Puncture two of the coconut eyes with a screwdriver and drain the milk out from the shell.

2 Crack the coconut shell, prise away the flesh, and then coarsely grate the coconut into a medium-size bowl.

COOK'S TIP

When buying a fresh coconut, check its freshness by shaking gently – you should hear the liquid swishing about inside. If not, it's dried out and stale.

3 Cut the rind from the pineapple with a sharp knife and remove the eyes with a potato peeler. Finely chop the flesh and add to the coconut together with any juice.

4 Halve the chillies lengthways and remove the stalks, seeds and membrane. Chop very finely and stir into the coconut mixture.

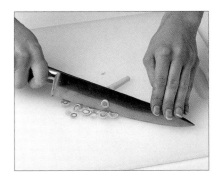

5 Finely chop the lemon grass with a very sharp knife. Add to the coconut mixture and stir in.

6 Add the remaining ingredients and stir well. Spoon into a serving dish and garnish with coriander sprigs.

Fiery Citrus Salsa

THIS VERY UNUSUAL SALSA makes a fantastic marinade for shellfish, and it is also delicious drizzled over chargrilled meat.

Serves 4

INGREDIENTS

1 orange
1 green apple
2 fresh red chillies, halved and seeded
1 garlic clove
8 fresh mint leaves
juice of 1 lemon
salt and ground black pepper

1 Slice the base off the orange so that it will stand firmly on a chopping board. Using a sharp knife, remove the peel by slicing from the top to the base of the orange.

2 Hold the orange in one hand over a bowl. Slice towards the middle of the fruit, to one side of a segment, and then gently twist the knife to ease the segment away from the membrane and out of the orange. Remove all the segments. Squeeze any juice from the remaining membrane into the bowl.

3 Peel the apple, slice it into wedges and remove the core.

4 Place the chillies in a blender or food processor with the orange segments and juice, apple wedges, garlic and fresh mint. Process for a few seconds until smooth. Then, with the motor running, slowly pour the lemon juice into the mixture.

5 Season to taste with a little salt and ground black pepper. Pour the salsa mixture into a bowl or small jug (pitcher) and serve immediately.

VARIATION

If you're feeling really fiery, don't seed the chillies! The seeds will make the salsa particularly hot and fierce.

Sweet Pepper Salsa

ROASTING PEPPERS ENHANCES their sweet flavour, making them perfect for salsas. This is delicious served with poached salmon.

Serves 4

INGREDIENTS

1 red (bell) pepper
1 yellow (bell) pepper
5ml/1 tsp cumin seeds
1 red chilli, seeded
30ml/2 tbsp chopped fresh coriander
  (cilantro) leaves, plus extra to garnish
30ml/2 tbsp olive oil
15ml/1 tbsp red wine vinegar
salt and ground black pepper

1 Preheat the grill (broiler) to medium. Place the peppers on a baking sheet and grill (broil) them for 8–10 minutes, turning regularly, until blackened and blistered.

2 Place the peppers in a bowl and cover with a clean dishtowel. Leave for 5 minutes so the steam helps to lift the skin away from the flesh. Remove the dishtowel.

3 Meanwhile, place the cumin seeds in a small frying pan. Heat gently, stirring, until the seeds start to splutter and release their aroma. Remove the pan from the heat, then tip out the seeds into a mortar and crush them lightly with a pestle.

4 When the peppers are cool enough to handle, pierce a hole in the base of each and squeeze out all of the juices into a bowl. Peel and seed the peppers, then process the flesh and juices in a blender or food processor with the chilli and coriander until finely chopped.

5 Stir in the oil, vinegar and cumin with salt and pepper to taste. Serve the salsa at room temperature, garnished with coriander.

COOK'S TIP

Choose red, yellow or orange peppers for this salsa, as green ones are less ripe and therefore not so sweet.

Pineapple and Passion Fruit Salsa

PILE THIS SWEET, FRUITY salsa into brandy snap baskets or meringue nests for a luxurious dessert.

Serves 6

INGREDIENTS

1 small fresh pineapple
2 passion fruit
150ml/¼ pint/⅔ cup Greek (US strained
    plain) yogurt
30ml/2 tbsp light muscovado
    (brown) sugar

3 Halve the passion fruit and use a spoon to scoop out the seeds and pulp into a bowl.

4 Stir in the chopped pineapple and the Greek yogurt. Cover and chill until required.

5 Stir in the muscovado sugar just before serving the salsa.

VARIATION

Lightly whipped double (heavy) cream can be used instead of the yogurt.

1 Cut off the top and bottom of the pineapple so that it will stand firmly on a chopping board. Using a large, sharp knife, slice off the peel.

2 Use a small, sharp knife to carefully cut out the eyes. Slice the peeled pineapple and use a small pastry cutter to cut out the tough core. Finely chop the flesh.

Plantain Salsa

HERE IS A SUMMERY SALSA which is perfect for lazy outdoor eating. Serve with barbecued or grilled meat or fish, or with taco chips for dipping.

Serves 4

INGREDIENTS
knob (pat) of butter
4 ripe plantains
handful of fresh coriander (cilantro), plus extra to garnish
30ml/2 tbsp olive oil
5ml/1 tsp cayenne pepper
salt and ground black pepper

COOK'S TIP

Be sure to choose ripe plantains with blackened skins for this recipe as they will be at their sweetest and most tender.

1 Preheat the oven to 200°C/400°F/Gas 6.

2 Grease 4 pieces of foil, each measuring roughly 15 x 20cm/6 x 8in, with the butter.

3 Peel the plantains and place 1 on each piece of buttered foil. Carefully fold the pieces of foil over the plantain sealing them tightly to form 4 parcels.

4 Bake the plantain for 25 minutes, or until tender. Alternatively, the plantain may be cooked in the embers of a charcoal barbecue.

5 Allow the parcels to cool slightly, then remove the plantains, discarding any liquid, and place in a food processor or blender.

6 Process the plantains with the coriander until fairly smooth. Stir in the olive oil, cayenne pepper, and salt and pepper to taste.

7 Serve immediately as the salsa will discolour and over-thicken if left to cool for too long. Garnish with torn coriander leaves.

Sweetcorn Salsa

SERVE THIS SUCCULENT SALSA with smoked meats or a cured gammon or ham steak.

Serves 4

INGREDIENTS

2 corn cobs
30ml/2 tbsp melted butter
4 tomatoes
6 spring onions (scallions), finely chopped
1 garlic clove, finely chopped
30ml/2 tbsp fresh lemon juice
30ml/2 tbsp olive oil
red Tabasco sauce, to taste
salt and ground black pepper
spring onion (scallion) slices, to garnish

1 Remove the husks and silky threads covering the corn cobs. Brush the cobs with the melted butter and gently cook on a barbecue or grill (broil) for 20–30 minutes, turning occasionally, until tender and tinged brown.

2 To remove the kernels, stand the cob upright on a chopping board and use a large, heavy knife to slice down the length of the cob.

3 Skewer the tomatoes in turn on a metal fork and hold in a gas flame for 1–2 minutes, turning, until the skin splits and wrinkles. Slip off the skin and dice the tomato flesh.

4 Mix the spring onions and garlic with the corn and tomato in a small bowl.

5 Mix the lemon juice, olive oil and Tabasco together. Season to taste.

6 Pour this over the salsa and stir well. Cover the salsa and leave to steep at room temperature for 1–2 hours before serving, garnished with slices of spring onion.

COOK'S TIP

Make this salsa in late summer when fresh cobs of corn are readily available and at the peak of their flavour.

Berry Salsa

This unusual fruit salsa is perfect to serve with grilled or barbecued fish or poultry.

Serves 4

INGREDIENTS
1 fresh jalapeño pepper
½ red onion, minced (ground)
2 spring onions (scallions), chopped
1 tomato, finely diced
1 small yellow (bell) pepper, seeded and minced (ground)
45ml/3 tbsp chopped coriander (cilantro)
1.5ml/¼ tsp salt
15ml/1 tbsp raspberry vinegar
15ml/1 tbsp fresh orange juice
5ml/1 tsp honey
15ml/1 tbsp olive oil
175g/6oz/1½ cups strawberries, hulled
175g/6oz/1½ cups blueberries or blackberries
200g/7oz/generous 1 cup raspberries

1 Wearing rubber gloves, finely chop the jalapeño pepper (discard the seeds and membrane if a less hot flavour is desired). Place the pepper in a medium-size bowl.

2 Add the red onion, spring onions, tomato, pepper and coriander, and stir well.

3 In a small bowl, whisk together the salt, vinegar, orange juice, honey and olive oil. Pour over the jalapeño mixture and stir well.

4 Coarsely chop the strawberries. Add to the jalapeño mixture with the other berries and stir to blend.

5 Allow to stand at room temperature for 3 hours, then serve.

COOK'S TIP

Thawed frozen berries can be used in the salsa, but the texture will be softer.

Mixed Melon Salsa

A COMBINATION OF TWO very different melons gives this salsa an exciting flavour and texture. Try it with thinly sliced prosciutto or smoked salmon.

Serves 10

INGREDIENTS

1 small orange-fleshed melon, such as Charentais
1 large wedge watermelon
2 oranges

VARIATION

Other melons can be used for this salsa. Try cantaloupe, Galia or Ogen.

1 Quarter the orange-fleshed melon and remove the seeds. Use a large, sharp knife to cut off the skin. Dice the melon flesh.

2 Pick out the seeds from the watermelon, then remove the skin. Dice the flesh into small chunks.

3 Use a zester to pare long strips of rind from both oranges. Halve the oranges and squeeze out all their juice.

4 Mix both types of the melon and the orange rind and juice together in a bowl. Chill for about 30 minutes and serve.

Pepper and Ginger Salsa

CHARGRILLING TO REMOVE the skins will take away any bitterness from the peppers and soften the flesh. Serve the salsa with meat or vegetable kebabs.

Serves 6

INGREDIENTS

1 large red (bell) pepper
1 large yellow (bell) pepper
1 large orange (bell) pepper
2.5ml/½ tsp coriander seeds
5ml/1 tsp cumin seeds
2.5cm/1in piece fresh root ginger, chopped
1 small garlic clove, chopped
30ml/2 tbsp lime or lemon juice
1 small red onion, finely chopped
30ml/2 tbsp fresh coriander
   (cilantro), chopped
5ml/1 tsp fresh thyme, chopped
salt and ground black pepper

1 Preheat the grill (broiler). Quarter the peppers and remove the stalks, membranes and seeds. Grill (broil), skin-side up, until charred and blistered. Rub off the skins and slice.

COOK'S TIP

If you don't have a pestle and mortar, crush the garlic and grate the ginger. The spices can be ground in a pepper mill or crushed with a rolling pin.

2 Over a moderate heat, gently dry-fry the coriander and cumin for 30 seconds to 1 minute, shaking the pan to make sure they don't scorch.

3 Crush the spices in a mortar with a pestle. Add the ginger and garlic and continue to work to a pulp. Work in the lime or lemon juice.

4 Mix together the peppers, spice mixture, onion and herbs. Season to taste with salt and ground black pepper and spoon into a serving bowl. Chill for 1–2 hours before serving as an accompaniment to meat or vegetable kebabs.

Orange and Chive Salsa

FRESH CHIVES AND SWEET oranges provide a refreshing combination of flavours. This salsa can be used to cool down spicy meat or poultry.

Serves 4

INGREDIENTS
2 large oranges
1 beefsteak tomato
bunch of fresh chives
1 garlic clove, thinly sliced
30ml/2 tbsp olive oil
sea salt

1 Slice the base off one orange so that it will stand firmly on a chopping board. Using a large, sharp knife, remove the peel by slicing from the top to the base of the orange.

2 Hold the orange over a bowl. Slice towards the middle of the fruit, to one side of a segment, and then twist the knife to ease the segment away from the membrane and out of the orange. Repeat to remove all segments. Squeeze any juice from the membrane.

3 Prepare the second orange in the same way. Roughly chop the orange segments and place them in the bowl with the collected juice.

4 Halve the tomato and use a teaspoon to scoop the seeds into the bowl. Finely dice the flesh and add it to the oranges, juice and seeds in the bowl.

5 Hold the bunch of chives together and use a pair of scissors to snip them into the bowl. Stir in the garlic.

6 Pour the olive oil over, season with sea salt to taste and stir well to mix. Serve within 2 hours.

Mango and Red Onion Salsa

A VERY SIMPLE TROPICAL salsa, which is livened up by the addition of passion fruit pulp. This salsa goes well with salmon and poultry.

Serves 4

INGREDIENTS

1 large ripe mango
1 red onion
2 passion fruit
6 large fresh basil leaves
juice of 1 lime, to taste
sea salt

1 Holding the mango upright on a chopping board, use a large knife to slice the flesh away from each side of the large flat stone (pit) in 2 pieces.

2 Using a smaller knife, trim away any flesh still clinging to the top and bottom of the stone.

3 Score the flesh of the mango halves deeply, taking care to avoid cutting through the skin: make parallel incisions about 1 cm/½ in apart; turn and cut lines in the opposite direction.

4 Carefully turn the skin inside out so the flesh stands out. Slice the dice away from the skin. Place in a bowl.

5 Finely chop the red onion and place it in the bowl with the mango. Halve the passion fruit, scoop out the seeds and pulp, and add to the mango mixture in the bowl.

6 Tear the basil leaves coarsely and stir them into the mixture with lime juice and a little sea salt to taste. Mix well and serve the salsa immediately.

VARIATION

Freshly cooked sweetcorn kernels are a delicious addition to this salsa.

Aromatic Peach and Cucumber Salsa

ANGOSTURA BITTERS ADD AN unusual and very pleasing flavour to this salsa. The distinctive, sweet taste of the mint complements chicken and other meat dishes.

Serves 4

INGREDIENTS
2 peaches
1 mini cucumber
2.5ml/½ tsp angostura bitters
15ml/1 tbsp olive oil
10ml/2 tsp fresh lemon juice
30ml/2 tbsp chopped fresh mint
salt and ground black pepper

1 Using a small, sharp knife, carefully score a line right around the centre of each peach, taking care to cut just through the skin.

2 Bring a large pan of water to the boil. Add the peaches and blanch them for 1 minute. Drain and briefly refresh in cold water. Peel off and discard the skin. Halve the peaches and remove their stones (pits). Finely dice the flesh and place in a bowl.

3 Trim the ends off the cucumber, then finely dice the flesh and stir it into the peaches. Stir the angostura bitters, olive oil and lemon juice together and then stir this dressing into the peach mixture.

VARIATION

Use diced mango in place of the peaches for an alternative.

4 Stir in the mint with salt and pepper to taste. Chill and serve within 1 hour.

COOK'S TIP

The texture of the peach and the crispness of the cucumber will fade fairly rapidly, so try to prepare this salsa as close to the serving time as possible.

Dips

Far from being just for parties, dips are for any occasion, any time of day, and any season. They are an opportunity for informal eating, an appetite teaser, and a very healthy way to snack. They're also a good choice for packed lunches and picnics, as they travel well and can be served in so many ways.

Hot or cold, dips are a very versatile food; they are invariably quick to make and uncomplicated, so they're easily rustled up at a moment's notice. For a satisfying treat, try a warm, creamy cheese Fonduta with crusty bread for dipping, or Hot Chilli Bean Dip. Or, as a light, refreshing summer snack, Blue Cheese Dip or creamy Guacamole with fresh crudités will fit the bill. For parties, choose a selection of different dips for variety, so there's something for everyone's taste.

Serve your favourite dips with raw vegetable crudités such as carrot, cucumber or celery sticks, raw mushrooms or cauliflower florets. Cooked vegetables such as asparagus or artichokes or deep-fried mushrooms seem incomplete without a creamy or tangy savoury dip. Or, try dipping fingers of pitta breads, breadsticks and taco chips, which are perfect for easy snacking.

Saffron Dip

SERVE THIS MILD DIP with fresh vegetable crudités — it is particularly good with florets of cauliflower.

Serves 4

INGREDIENTS

15ml/1 tbsp boiling water
small pinch of saffron threads
200g/7oz/scant 1 cup fromage frais
  or cream cheese
10 fresh chives
10 fresh basil leaves
salt and ground black pepper

VARIATION

Leave out the saffron and add a squeeze of lemon or lime juice instead. A pinch of ground turmeric gives a good colour.

2 Beat the fromage frais or cream cheese until smooth, then stir in the saffron liquid.

3 Use a pair of scissors to snip the chives into the dip. Tear the basil leaves into small pieces and stir them in.

1 Pour the boiling water into a small bowl and add the saffron threads. Leave to steep for 3 minutes.

4 Add salt and pepper to taste. Serve the dip immediately.

Basil and Lemon Mayonnaise

THIS FRESH MAYONNAISE is flavoured with lemon and two types of basil. Serve as a dip with potato wedges or crudités, or as an accompaniment to salads and baked potatoes.

Serves 4

INGREDIENTS

2 large (US extra large) egg yolks
15ml/1 tbsp lemon juice
150ml/¼ pint/⅔ cup olive oil
150ml/¼ pint/⅔ cup sunflower oil
handful of green basil leaves
handful of dark opal (purple) basil leaves
4 garlic cloves, crushed
salt and ground black pepper
green and dark opal (purple) basil leaves
    and sea salt, to garnish

COOK'S TIP

Dark opal basil has crinkled, deep-purple leaves and a richly scented flavour, with a hint of blackcurrants.

1 Place the egg yolks and lemon juice in a food processor or blender and process them briefly together.

2 In a jug (pitcher), stir the two oils together. With the machine running, pour in the oil very slowly, a drop at a time.

3 Once half the oil has been added, the remainder can be incorporated more quickly. Continue processing the mixture to form a thick and creamy mayonnaise.

4 Tear both types of basil into small pieces and stir into the mayonnaise with the crushed garlic and seasoning. Transfer to a serving dish, cover and chill until ready to serve, garnished with basil leaves and sea salt.

Blue Cheese Dip

2 Add the soft cheese and beat well to blend the two cheeses together.

3 Gradually beat in the yogurt, adding enough to give you the consistency you prefer.

THIS DIP CAN BE mixed up in next to no time and is delicious served with pears, or with fresh vegetable crudités. Add more yogurt to make a great dressing. This is a very thick dip to which you can add a little more yogurt or a little milk for a softer consistency.

Serves 4

INGREDIENTS

150g/5oz blue cheese, such as Stilton or Danish blue
150g/5oz/⅔ cup soft cheese
75ml/5 tbsp Greek (US strained plain) yogurt
salt and ground black pepper

1 Crumble the blue cheese into a bowl. Using a wooden spoon, beat the cheese to soften it.

4 Season with lots of black pepper and a little salt. Chill the dip until you are ready to serve it.

Mellow Garlic Dip

TWO WHOLE HEADS OF garlic may seem like a lot, but roasting transforms the flesh to a tender, sweet and mellow pulp. Serve with crunchy breadstick or tortilla chips. For a low-fat version of this dip, use reduced-fat mayonnaise and low-fat yogurt.

Serves 4

INGREDIENTS

2 whole garlic heads
15ml/1 tbsp olive oil
60ml/4 tbsp mayonnaise
75ml/5 tbsp Greek (US strained plain) yogurt
5ml/1 tsp wholegrain mustard
salt and ground black pepper

1 Preheat the oven to 200°C/400°F/ Gas 6. Separate the garlic cloves and place them in a small roasting pan.

2 Pour the olive oil over the garlic cloves and turn them with a spoon to coat them evenly. Roast them for 20–30 minutes, or until tender and softened. Leave to cool for 5 minutes.

3 Trim off the root end of each roasted garlic clove. Peel the cloves and discard the skins. Place the roasted garlic on a chopping board and sprinkle with salt. Mash with a fork until puréed.

4 Place the garlic in a small bowl and stir in the mayonnaise, yogurt and wholegrain mustard.

5 Check and adjust the seasoning, then spoon the dip into a bowl. Cover and chill until ready to serve.

COOK'S TIP

If you are cooking on a barbecue, leave the garlic heads whole and cook until tender, turning occasionally. Peel and mash.

Butternut Squash and Parmesan Dip

THE RICH, NUTTY FLAVOUR of butternut squash is enhanced by roasting. Serve this dip with Melba toast or cheese straws.

Serves 4

INGREDIENTS
1 butternut squash
15g/½oz/1 tbsp butter
4 garlic cloves, unpeeled
30ml/2 tbsp freshly grated
   Parmesan cheese
45–75ml/3–5 tbsp double (heavy) cream
salt and ground black pepper

1 Preheat the oven to 200°C/400°F/ Gas 6.

2 Halve the butternut squash, then scoop out and discard the seeds.

3 Use a small, sharp knife to deeply score the flesh in a criss-cross pattern: cut as close to the skin as possible, without cutting through it.

4 Arrange both halves in a small roasting pan and dot them with the butter. Sprinkle the butternut squash with salt and ground black pepper and roast on a high heat near the top of the oven for 20 minutes.

5 Tuck the unpeeled garlic cloves around the squash in the roasting pan and continue roasting for 20 minutes, until the butternut squash is tender and softened.

6 Scoop the flesh out of the squash shells and place it in a food processor or blender. Slip the garlic cloves out of their skins and add to the squash. Process until smooth.

7 With the motor running, add all but 15ml/1 tbsp of the Parmesan cheese and then the cream. Check the seasoning and spoon the dip into a serving bowl; it is at its best served warm. Sprinkle the reserved cheese over the top. If you don't have a food processor or blender, mash the squash in a bowl using a potato masher, then beat in the cheese and cream with a wooden spoon.

VARIATION

Try making this dip with pumpkin or other types of squash, such as acorn squash or New Zealand kabocha. Adjust the cooking time depending on size.

Thousand Island Dip

This variation on the classic dressing is far removed from the original version, but can be served in the same way – with fish and shellfish laced on to bamboo skewers for dipping or with a mixed shellfish salad.

Serves 4

INGREDIENTS

4 sun-dried tomatoes in oil
4 tomatoes
150g/5oz/²⁄₃ cup soft (farmer's) cheese
60ml/4 tbsp mayonnaise
30ml/2 tbsp tomato purée (paste)
30ml/2 tbsp chopped fresh parsley
grated rind and juice of 1 lemon
red Tabasco sauce, to taste
5ml/1 tsp Worcestershire or soy sauce
salt and ground black pepper

1 Drain the sun-dried tomatoes on kitchen paper to remove excess oil, then finely chop them.

2 Skewer each tomato in turn on a metal fork and hold in a gas flame for 1–2 minutes, or until the skin wrinkles and splits. Allow to cool, then slip off and discard the skins. Halve the tomatoes and scoop out the seeds with a teaspoon. Finely chop the tomato flesh and set aside.

3 In a bowl, beat the soft cheese, then gradually beat in the mayonnaise and tomato purée to a smooth mixture.

4 Stir in the chopped parsley and sun-dried tomatoes, then add the chopped tomatoes and their seeds, and mix well.

5 Add the lemon rind and juice and Tabasco sauce to taste. Stir in the Worcestershire or soy sauce, and salt and pepper to taste.

6 Transfer the dip to a serving bowl, cover and chill until ready to serve.

VARIATION

Stir in cayenne pepper or a chopped fresh chilli for a more fiery dip. Garnish with a small piece of lemon, if you like.

Guacamole

THIS IS QUITE A fiery version of the popular Mexican dish, although probably nowhere near as hot as the dish you would be served in Mexico, where it often seems that heat knows no bounds! Serve it as a snack with tortilla chips or breadsticks.

Serves 4

INGREDIENTS

2 ripe avocados
2 tomatoes, peeled, seeded and
    finely chopped
6 spring onions (scallions), finely chopped
1–2 chillies, seeded and finely chopped
30ml/2 tbsp fresh lime or lemon juice
15ml/1 tbsp chopped fresh
    coriander (cilantro)
salt and ground black pepper
fresh coriander (cilantro) sprigs, to garnish

1 Cut the avocados in half and remove the stones (pits) and discard. Scoop the flesh into a large bowl and mash it roughly with a large fork.

COOK'S TIP

Unless you are going to serve the dip immediately, cover the surface closely with a piece of clear film (plastic wrap) to prevent browning. If the surface should still start to brown, stir the dip lightly before serving.

2 Add the tomatoes, spring onions, chillies, lime or lemon juice and coriander. Mix well and season with salt and ground black pepper to taste.

3 Serve as soon as possible, garnished with fresh coriander sprigs.

VARIATION

For extra flavour, stir in a crushed garlic clove, or season with garlic salt.

Spiced Carrot Dip

THIS IS A DELICIOUS dip with a sweet and spicy flavour. Serve wheat crackers or fiery tortilla chips as accompaniments for dipping.

Serves 4

INGREDIENTS

1 onion
3 carrots, plus extra to garnish
grated rind and juice of 2 oranges
15ml/1 tbsp hot curry paste
150ml/¼ pint/⅔ cup natural (plain) yogurt
handful of fresh basil leaves
15–30ml/1–2 tbsp fresh lemon juice,
  to taste
red Tabasco sauce, to taste
salt and ground black pepper

3 Stir in the yogurt. Tear the basil leaves into small pieces and add most of them to the carrot mixture.

4 Add the lemon juice, Tabasco and seasoning. Serve within a few hours at room temperature, garnished with grated carrot and basil.

VARIATION

Greek (US strained plain) yogurt or sour cream may be used in place of the natural yogurt to make a richer, creamier textured dip.

1 Finely chop the onion. Peel and grate the carrots. Place the onion, carrots, orange rind and juice, and curry paste in a small pan. Bring to the boil, cover and simmer for 10 minutes.

2 Process the mixture in a blender or food processor until smooth. Leave to cool.

Creamy Aubergine Dip

SPREAD THIS VELVET-TEXTURED DIP thickly on to toasted rounds of bread, then top them with slivers of sun-dried tomato to make wonderful, Italian-style crostini.

Serves 4

INGREDIENTS

1 large aubergine (eggplant)
30ml/2 tbsp olive oil
1 small onion, finely chopped
2 garlic cloves, finely chopped
60ml/4 tbsp chopped fresh parsley
75ml/5 tbsp crème fraîche
red Tabasco sauce, to taste
juice of 1 lemon, to taste
salt and ground black pepper

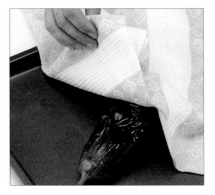

1 Preheat the grill (broiler) to medium. Place the aubergine on a non-stick baking sheet and grill (broil) it for 20–30 minutes under a medium-high heat, turning occasionally, until the skin is blackened and wrinkled, and the aubergine feels soft when squeezed.

2 Cover the aubergine with a clean dishtowel and leave it to cool for about 5 minutes.

3 Heat the oil in a frying pan and cook the onion and garlic for 5 minutes, until they are softened, but not browned.

4 Peel the skin from the aubergine. Mash the flesh with a large fork to make a pulpy purée.

5 Stir in the onion and garlic, parsley and crème fraîche. Add Tabasco, lemon juice, and salt and pepper to taste.

6 Transfer the dip to a serving bowl and serve warm or leave to cool and serve at room temperature.

COOK'S TIP

The aubergine can be roasted in the oven at 200°C/400°F/Gas 6 for 20 minutes, or until tender, if preferred.

Hot Chilli Bean Dip

MAKE THIS ONE AS hot as you like –
the sour cream helps to balance the
heat of the chillies.

Serves 4

INGREDIENTS

275g/10oz/1½ cups dried pinto beans,
   soaked overnight and drained
1 bay leaf
45ml/3 tbsp sea salt
15ml/1 tbsp vegetable oil
1 small onion, sliced
1 garlic clove, minced (ground)
2–4 canned hot green chillies (optional)
75ml/5 tbsp sour cream, plus extra
   to garnish
2.5ml/½ tsp ground cumin
hot pepper sauce, to taste
15ml/1 tbsp chopped fresh
   coriander (cilantro)

1 Place the beans in a large pan. Add fresh cold water to cover and the bay leaf. Bring to a boil, then cover, and simmer for 30 minutes.

2 Add the sea salt and continue simmering for about 30 minutes, or until the beans are tender.

3 Drain the cooked beans, reserving 120ml/4fl oz/½ cup of the liquid. Let cool slightly. Discard the bay leaf.

4 Heat the oil in a non-stick frying pan. Add the onion and garlic and cook over low heat for 8–10 minutes, or until just softened, stirring occasionally.

5 In a food processor or blender, combine the beans, onion mixture, chillies, if using, and the reserved cooking liquid. Process until the mixture is a coarse purée.

6 Transfer to a bowl and stir in the sour cream, cumin, and hot pepper sauce to taste. Stir in the coriander, garnish with sour cream, and serve warm.

VARIATION

*To save time, use 2½ x 400g/14oz cans
beans instead of the dried beans.*

Hummus

2 Add the tahini or peanut butter, and process until fairly smooth. With the motor still running, slowly pour in the oil and lemon juice.

3 Stir in the cayenne pepper and add more salt to taste. If the mixture is too thick, stir in a little cold water. Transfer the purée to a serving bowl.

THIS NUTRITIOUS DIP CAN be served with vegetable crudités or packed into salad-filled pitta, but it is best spread thickly on hot buttered toast. Tahini is a thick, smooth and oily paste made from sesame seeds. It is a classic ingredient in this Middle-Eastern dip.

Serves 4

INGREDIENTS

400g/14oz can chickpeas, drained
2 garlic cloves
30ml/2 tbsp tahini or smooth peanut butter
60ml/4 tbsp olive oil
juice of 1 lemon
2.5ml/½ tsp cayenne pepper
15ml/1 tbsp sesame seeds
sea salt

1 Rinse the chickpeas well and place in a food processor or blender with the garlic and a good pinch of sea salt. Process until very finely chopped.

4 Heat a small non-stick pan and add the sesame seeds. Cook them for 2–3 minutes, shaking the pan, until they are golden brown in colour. Allow them to cool, then sprinkle them over the purée.

Cannellini Bean Dip

THIS SOFT BEAN DIP or pâté is good spread on wheaten crackers or toasted muffins. Alternatively, it can be served with wedges of tomato and a crisp green salad.

Serves 4

INGREDIENTS
400g/14oz can cannellini beans
grated rind and juice of 1 lemon
30ml/2 tbsp olive oil
1 garlic clove, finely chopped
30ml/2 tbsp chopped fresh parsley
red Tabasco sauce, to taste
salt and ground black pepper
cayenne pepper, to garnish

1 Drain the beans and rinse them well under cold water. Drain well and transfer to a bowl.

2 Use a potato masher to roughly purée the beans, then stir in the lemon rind, juice and olive oil.

3 Stir in the chopped garlic and parsley. Add Tabasco sauce, salt and pepper to taste.

4 Spoon the mixture into a small bowl and dust lightly with cayenne pepper. Chill until ready to serve.

VARIATION

Canned or cooked butter (lima) beans or red kidney beans can also be used for this dip.

Sour Cream Cooler

THIS COOLING DIP MAKES the perfect accompaniment to hot and spicy Mexican dishes. Alternatively, serve it as a snack with the fieriest tortilla chips you can find.

Serves 2

INGREDIENTS

1 small yellow (bell) pepper

2 small tomatoes

30ml/2 tbsp chopped fresh parsley, plus extra to garnish

150ml/¼ pint/⅔ cup sour cream

grated lemon rind, to garnish

1 Halve the pepper lengthways. With a sharp knife, remove the core and scoop out the seeds, then cut the flesh into tiny dice.

2 Cut the tomatoes in half, then use a teaspoon to scoop out and discard the seeds. Cut the tomato flesh into tiny dice.

3 Stir the pepper and tomato dice and the chopped parsley into the sour cream and mix well.

4 Spoon the dip into a small bowl and chill. Garnish with grated lemon rind and parsley before serving.

VARIATION

Use finely diced avocado or cucumber in place of the pepper or tomato.

Tzatziki

THIS CLASSIC GREEK DIP is a cooling mix of yogurt, cucumber and mint, perfect for a hot summer's day. Serve it with strips of lightly toasted pitta bread.

Serves 4

INGREDIENTS

1 mini cucumber
4 spring onions (scallions)
1 garlic clove
200ml/7fl oz/scant 1 cup Greek
   (US strained plain) yogurt
45ml/3 tbsp chopped fresh mint
salt and ground black pepper
fresh mint sprig, to garnish (optional)

1 Trim the ends from the cucumber, then cut it into 5mm/¼in dice. Set aside.

2 Trim the spring onions and garlic, then chop both finely.

COOK'S TIP

Choose Greek yogurt for this dip – it gives it a deliciously rich, creamy texture.

3 Beat the yogurt until smooth, if necessary, then gently stir in the cucumber, spring onions, garlic and mint.

4 Add salt and plenty of ground black pepper to taste, then transfer the mixture to a serving bowl. Chill until ready to serve and then garnish with a small mint sprig, if liked.

Red Onion Raita

RAITA IS A TRADITIONAL Indian side
dish served as an accompaniment
for hot curries. It is also delicious
served with poppadums as a dip.

Serves 4

INGREDIENTS

5ml/1 tsp cumin seeds
1 small garlic clove
1 small green chilli
1 large red onion
150ml/¼ pint/⅔ cup natural (plain) yogurt
30ml/2 tbsp chopped fresh coriander
(cilantro), plus extra to garnish
2.5ml/½ tsp sugar
salt

1 Heat a small frying pan and dry-fry the cumin seeds for 1–2 minutes, until they release their aroma and begin to pop.

VARIATION

*For an extra tangy raita stir in 15ml/
1 tbsp lemon juice.*

2 Lightly crush the seeds in a mortar with a pestle or flatten them with the heel of a heavy-bladed knife.

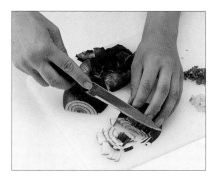

3 Finely chop the garlic. Remove the fiery seeds from the chilli and chop the flesh finely, along with the red onion.

4 Place the natural yogurt in a bowl and add the garlic, chilli and red onion, along with the crushed cumin seeds and fresh coriander. Stir to combine.

5 Add sugar and salt to taste. Spoon the raita into a small bowl and chill until ready to serve. Garnish with extra coriander before serving.

Satay Dip

A DELICIOUSLY PUNGENT SAUCE which tastes great served with spicy chicken on skewers but is equally good as a dip for crisp vegetables.

Serves 6

INGREDIENTS

150g/5oz/1¼ cup roasted,
  unsalted peanuts
45ml/3 tbsp vegetable oil
1 small onion, roughly chopped
2 garlic cloves, crushed
1 red chilli, seeded and chopped
2.5cm/1in piece fresh root ginger, peeled
  and chopped
5cm/2in piece lemon grass,
  roughly chopped
2.5ml/½ tsp ground cumin
45ml/3 tbsp chopped fresh coriander
  (cilantro) stalks
15ml/1 tbsp sesame oil
175ml/6fl oz/¾ cup coconut milk
30ml/2 tbsp thick soy sauce (kecap manis)
10ml/2 tsp lime juice
salt and ground black pepper
lime wedges and chives, to garnish

1 Rub the husks from the peanuts in a clean dishtowel.

2 Place the nuts in a food processor or blender with 30ml/2 tbsp vegetable oil, and process to a smooth paste. Transfer to a bowl.

3 Place the next 7 ingredients in the food processor or blender and process to a fairly smooth paste.

4 Heat the remaining vegetable oil with the sesame oil in a frying pan and add the onion paste. Cook over a low heat for about 10–15 minutes, stirring occasionally.

5 Stir in the peanuts, coconut milk, soy sauce and lime juice, and keep stirring while it heats through.

6 Add salt and ground black pepper to taste, then spoon the mixture into small bowls or saucers. Serve warm, garnished with lime wedges and chives.

Spicy Tuna Dip

2 Halve the eggs, remove the yolks and then place in a food processor or blender. Discard the whites or use in another dish.

3 Reserve a few olives for garnishing, then add the rest to the processor or blender together with the remaining ingredients. Process together until smooth. Season with pepper to taste.

A PIQUANT DIP, DELICIOUS served with breadsticks – use more oil for a sauce, less for filling boiled eggs or fresh tomatoes.

Serves 6

INGREDIENTS

90g/3¹/₄oz can tuna fish in oil
olive oil
3 hard-boiled (hard-cooked) eggs
75g/3oz/³/₄ cup pitted green olives
50g/2oz can anchovy fillets, drained
45ml/3 tbsp capers, drained
10ml/2 tsp Dijon mustard
ground black pepper
fresh parsley sprigs, to garnish

1 Drain the oil from the tuna into a small bowl and make up the quantity to 90ml/6 tbsp with olive oil.

4 Spoon into a bowl and garnish with the reserved olives and the parsley.

COOK'S TIP

Choose a good quality, light olive oil for this dip – richly flavoured extra virgin oils may dominate the flavour.

Lemon and Coconut Dhal

A WARM, SPICY DISH, this can be served either as a dip with poppadums or to accompany an Indian main dish.

Serves 8

INGREDIENTS
30ml/2 tbsp sunflower oil
5cm/2in piece fresh root ginger,
   finely chopped
1 onion, finely chopped
2 garlic cloves, finely chopped
2 small red chillies, seeded and
   finely chopped
5ml/1 tsp cumin seeds
150g/5oz/²/₃ cup red lentils
250ml/8fl oz/1 cup water
15ml/1 tbsp hot curry paste
200ml/7fl oz/scant 1 cup coconut cream
juice of 1 lemon
handful of fresh coriander (cilantro) leaves
25g/1oz/¹/₄ cup flaked (sliced) almonds
salt and ground black pepper

1 Heat the oil in a large, shallow pan. Add the chopped ginger, onion, garlic, chillies and the cumin seeds. Cook for 5 minutes, until softened but not coloured.

2 Stir the lentils, water and curry paste into the pan. Bring to the boil, cover and cook gently over a low heat for 15–20 minutes, stirring the mixture occasionally, until the lentils are just tender and not yet broken.

3 Stir in all but 30ml/2 tbsp of the coconut cream. Bring to the boil and cook, uncovered, for a further 15–20 minutes, or until thick and pulpy. Remove from the heat, then stir in the lemon juice and coriander. Add salt and pepper to taste.

VARIATION

Try making this dhal with yellow split peas: they take longer to cook and a little extra water has to be added but the result is equally tasty.

4 Heat a large pan and cook the flaked almonds for 1 or 2 minutes on each side until golden brown. Stir about three-quarters of the toasted almonds into the dhal.

5 Transfer the dhal to a serving bowl and swirl in the remaining coconut cream. Sprinkle the reserved almonds on top and serve warm.

Fonduta

FONTINA IS AN ITALIAN medium-fat cheese with a mild nutty flavour, which melts easily and smoothly. It is a little like Gruyère, which makes a good substitute. This delicious cheese dip needs only some warm ciabatta bread or focaccia, a crisp salad and some robust red wine to complete the meal.

Serves 4

INGREDIENTS

225g/8oz/2 cups diced Fontina cheese
250ml/8fl oz/1 cup milk
15g/½ oz/1 tbsp butter
2 eggs, lightly beaten
ground black pepper

1 Put the cheese in a bowl with the milk and leave to soak for 2–3 hours. Transfer to a double boiler or a heatproof bowl set over a pan of simmering water.

2 Add the butter and eggs and cook gently, stirring until the cheese has melted to a smooth sauce with the consistency of custard.

3 Remove from the heat and season with pepper. Transfer to a serving dish and serve immediately.

COOK'S TIP

Don't overheat the sauce, or the eggs might curdle. A very gentle heat will produce a lovely smooth sauce.

VARIATION

Pour the Fonduta over hot pasta or polenta for a really satisfying main dish.

Tahini Yogurt Dip with Sesame Seed-coated Falafel

SESAME SEEDS ARE USED to give a crunchy coating to these spicy bean patties. Serve with the tahini yogurt dip and warm pitta bread.

Serves 4

INGREDIENTS

250g/9oz/1⅓ cups dried chickpeas
2 garlic cloves, crushed
1 red chilli, seeded and finely sliced
5ml/1 tsp ground coriander
5ml/1 tsp ground cumin
15ml/1 tbsp chopped fresh mint
15ml/1 tbsp chopped fresh parsley
2 spring onions (scallions), finely chopped
1 large (US extra large) egg, beaten
sesame seeds, for coating
sunflower oil, for frying
salt and ground black pepper

For the tahini yogurt dip
30ml/2 tbsp light tahini
200g/7oz/scant 1 cup natural (plain)
    live yogurt
5ml/1 tsp cayenne pepper, plus extra
    for sprinkling
15ml/1 tbsp chopped fresh mint
1 spring onion (scallion), finely sliced

2 Meanwhile, make the tahini yogurt dip. Mix together the tahini, yogurt, cayenne pepper and mint in a small bowl. Sprinkle the spring onion and extra cayenne pepper on top and chill.

4 Form the chilled chickpea paste into 12 patties with your hands, then roll each one in the sesame seeds to coat thoroughly.

5 Heat enough oil to cover the base of a large frying pan. Fry the falafel, in batches if necessary, for 6 minutes, turning once.

VARIATION

The dip is also marvellous served with vegetable crisps (US chips).

1 Place the chickpeas in a bowl, cover with cold water and leave to soak overnight. Drain and rinse the chickpeas, then place in a pan and cover with cold water. Bring to the boil and boil rapidly for 10 minutes, then reduce the heat and simmer for 1½–2 hours, or until tender.

3 Combine the chickpeas with the garlic, chilli, ground spices, herbs, spring onions and seasoning, then mix in the egg. Place in a food processor and blend until the mixture forms a coarse paste. If the paste seems too soft, chill it for 30 minutes.

Papaya Dip with Fresh Fruit

SWEET AND SMOOTH PAPAYA teams up well with crème fraîche to make a luscious, tropical sweet dip which is very good with sweet biscuits, cookies or fresh fruit for dipping. If fresh coconut is not available, buy coconut strands and lightly toast in a hot oven until golden.

Serves 6

INGREDIENTS

2 ripe papayas
200ml/7fl oz/scant 1 cup crème fraîche
1 piece stem (crystallized) ginger
fresh coconut, to decorate
papaya or other fresh fruit, to serve

1 Halve the papayas lengthways, then scoop out and discard the seeds.

2 Scoop out the flesh and process it until smooth in a food processor or blender.

3 Stir in the crème fraîche and process until well blended. Finely chop the stem ginger and stir it in, then chill until ready to serve.

4 Pierce a hole in the "eye" of the coconut and drain off the liquid. Put the coconut in a plastic bag. Hold it securely in one hand and hit it sharply with a hammer.

5 Remove the shell from a piece of coconut, then snap the nut into pieces no wider than 2.5cm/1in.

6 Use a swivel-bladed vegetable peeler to shave off 2cm/¾in lengths of coconut. Scatter these over the dip. Serve with pieces of extra papaya or other fresh fruit.

Malted Chocolate and Banana Dip with Fresh Fruit

CHOCOLATE AND BANANA combine irresistibly in this rich dip, served with fresh fruit in season. For a creamier dip, stir in some lightly whipped cream just before serving.

Serves 4

INGREDIENTS

50g/2oz plain (semisweet) chocolate
2 large ripe bananas
15ml/1 tbsp malt extract
mixed fresh fruit, such as strawberries,
    peaches and kiwi fruit, halved or sliced,
    to serve

1 Break the chocolate into pieces and place in a small, heatproof bowl. Stand the bowl over a pan of gently simmering water and stir the chocolate occasionally until it melts. Allow to cool slightly.

2 Break the bananas into pieces and process in a food processor or blender until finely chopped.

3 With the motor running, pour in the malt extract, and continue processing the mixture until it is thick and frothy.

4 Drizzle in the chocolate in a steady stream and process until well blended. Serve immediately, with the prepared fruit alongside.

COOK'S TIP

This smooth dip can be prepared in advance and chilled.

Relishes and Chutneys

It's a myth that preserving is an art – the preparation of a simple chutney or relish is within the reach of any cook, and it's such a worthwhile task. When you line up the jars on your kitchen shelf – and maybe even give a few jars as gifts, you'll feel a real glow of satisfaction.

Once you open the jar, the benefits are even more evident – a spoonful of fruity, spicy chutney or relish can lift the appetite and transform the flavour of the plainest hunk of bread and cheese or meat into a tasty lunch. If your taste is for the exotic, Indian curries are traditionally accompanied by a spoonful of fruity chutney, often made with mangoes, and spiced with chilli or ginger.

Almost any cooked meat will benefit from a spicy spoonful of rich chutney on the side – every burger needs it's relish, and even a plateful of fresh oysters can be lifted to another level by adding a spoonful of Bloody Mary Relish.

The flavour of most chutneys and relishes improves with keeping, so, however tempting it may be, store them carefully for 3–4 weeks before opening the jar to enjoy them at their best.

Classic Quick Recipes

Curried Fruit Chutney

A PIQUANT FRUIT CHUTNEY that is delicious with cold sliced turkey and ham over the Christmas season – or at any time of year.

Makes about 1.2kg/2½lb

INGREDIENTS
225g/8oz/1 cup dried apricots
225g/8oz/1⅓ cups dried peaches
225g/8oz/1⅓ cups dates, stoned (pitted)
225g/8oz/1⅓ cups raisins
1–2 garlic cloves, crushed
225g/8oz/1 cup light muscovado
 (brown) sugar
300ml/½ pint/1¼ cups white
 malt vinegar
300ml/½ pint/1¼ cups water
5ml/1 tsp salt
10ml/2 tsp mild curry powder

1 Put all the ingredients in a large pan, cover and simmer very gently for 10–15 minutes, or until the mixture is tender.

2 Transfer the mixture to a food processor in batches and chop or mince (grind) coarsely.

3 Spoon the chutney into clean jam jars. Seal the jars and label them. Store in a cool place for 4 weeks before using.

Ginger, Date and Apple Chutney

SERVE THIS RICH, SPICY chutney with cold sliced meats or pies. Make it well ahead to allow time for the warming flavours to mature.

Makes about 1.6kg/3–3½lb

INGREDIENTS
450g/1lb cooking apples
450g/1lb/3¼ cups dates, stoned (pitted)
225g/8oz/1 cup dried apricots
115g/4oz glacé (candied) ginger, chopped
1–2 garlic cloves, crushed
225g/8oz/1⅓ cups sultanas
 (golden raisins)
225g/8oz/1 cup light muscovado
 (brown) sugar
5ml/1 tsp salt
300ml/½ pint/1¼ cups white malt vinegar

VARIATION

If you prefer, use drained pieces of preserved (stem) ginger in syrup.

1 Peel, core and chop the apples into small chunks. Roughly chop the dates and apricots.

2 Put all the fruit together in a large pan with all the remaining ingredients. Cover and simmer gently for 10–15 minutes, or until the fruit is tender and the liquid is well reduced.

3 Spoon into clean jam jars. Seal the jars and label them. Store in a cool place for 4 weeks before using.

Anchovy and Parsley Relish

ANCHOVIES AND PARSLEY make a flavourful relish to serve as a topping for fresh vegetables. Serve these fresh-tasting snacks as an appetizer to a rich meal, or with drinks.

Makes about 225g/8oz

INGREDIENTS

50g/2oz/2 cups flat leaf parsley
50g/2oz/½ cup black olives, pitted
25g/1oz/½ cup sun-dried tomatoes
4 canned anchovy fillets, drained
50g/2oz red onion, finely chopped
25g/1oz small pickled capers, rinsed
1 garlic clove, finely chopped
15ml/1 tbsp olive oil
juice of ½ lime
1.5ml/¼ tsp ground black pepper
a selection of cherry tomatoes, radishes,
*   celery and cucumber, to serve*

1 Coarsely chop the parsley, black olives, sun-dried tomatoes and anchovy fillets and mix in a bowl with the onion, capers, garlic, olive oil, lime juice and black pepper.

2 Halve the cherry tomatoes and radishes, chop the celery into bite-size chunks and cut the cucumber into 1cm/½ in slices. Top each of the prepared vegetables with a generous amount of relish and serve immediately.

Spiced Cranberry and Orange Relish

THIS COLOURFUL, FESTIVE RELISH is excellent served with roast turkey, goose or duck.

Makes about 450g/1lb

INGREDIENTS

225g/8oz/2 cups fresh cranberries
1 onion, finely chopped
150ml/¼ pint/⅔ cup port
115g/4oz/generous ½ cup caster
*   (superfine) sugar*
finely grated rind and juice of 1 orange
2.5ml/½ tsp English (hot) mustard powder
1.5ml/¼ tsp ground ginger
1.5ml/¼ tsp ground cinnamon
5ml/1 tsp cornflour (cornstarch)
50g/2oz/scant ½ cup raisins

COOK'S TIP

Frozen cranberries can be used instead of fresh – simply add them straight from the freezer.

1 Put the cranberries, onion, port and sugar in a pan. Cook the mixture gently for 10 minutes, or until tender.

2 Mix the orange juice, mustard powder, ginger, cinnamon and cornflour together. Stir them into the cranberries.

3 Add the raisins and orange rind. Allow to thicken over the heat, stirring, and then simmer for 2 minutes. Cool, cover and chill ready for serving.

Pickled Peach and Chilli Chutney

THIS IS A REALLY SPICY, rich chutney that is great served with cold roast meats or a strong farmhouse Cheddar cheese.

Makes about 450g/1lb

INGREDIENTS

475ml/16fl oz/2 cups cider vinegar
275g/10oz/1¼ cups light muscovado (brown) sugar
225g/8oz/1½ cups stoned (pitted) and finely chopped dried dates
5ml/1 tsp ground allspice
5ml/1 tsp ground mace
450g/1lb ripe peaches, stoned (pitted)
3 onions, thinly sliced
4 fresh red chillies, seeded and finely chopped
4 garlic cloves, crushed
5cm/2in piece of fresh root ginger, finely grated
5ml/1 tsp salt

1 Place the vinegar, sugar, chopped dates and spices in a large, heavy pan and bring to the boil over a medium heat, stirring occasionally.

2 Cut the peaches into small chunks. Add to the pan with all the remaining ingredients and return the mixture to the boil. Lower the heat and simmer for 40–50 minutes, or until thick. Stir frequently to prevent the mixture from burning on the base of the pan.

3 Spoon the chutney into clean, sterilized jars and seal. When cold, store the jars in the refrigerator and use within 2 months.

COOK'S TIP

To test the consistency of the finished chutney before bottling, spoon a little of the mixture on to a plate: the chutney is ready once it holds its shape.

Nectarine Relish

THIS SWEET AND TANGY fruit relish goes very well with hot roast meats such as pork, and game birds, such as guinea fowl and pheasant. Make it while nectarines are plentiful and keep covered in the refrigerator.

Makes about 450g/1lb

INGREDIENTS

45ml/3 tbsp olive oil
2 Spanish onions, thinly sliced
1 fresh green chilli, seeded and finely chopped
5ml/1 tsp finely chopped fresh rosemary
2 bay leaves
450g/1lb nectarines, stoned (pitted) and diced
150g/5oz/1 cup raisins
10ml/2 tsp crushed coriander seeds
350g/12 oz/1½ cups demerara (raw) sugar
200ml/7fl oz/scant 1 cup red wine vinegar

1 Heat the oil in a large, heavy pan. Add the sliced onions, chopped chilli and rosemary, and the bay leaves. Cook, stirring frequently, for 15–20 minutes, or until the onions are soft but not browned.

COOK'S TIP

Jars of this relish make a welcome gift. Add a colourful tag reminding the recipient to keep it in the refrigerator.

2 Add all the remaining ingredients and bring to the boil slowly, stirring often. Lower the heat and simmer for 1 hour, or until the relish is thick and sticky, stirring occasionally.

3 Remove and discard the bay leaves. Spoon into sterilized jars, and seal. Cool, then chill. The relish will keep in the refrigerator for up to 5 months.

Piquant Pineapple Relish

THIS FRUITY SWEET-AND-SOUR relish is excellent served with grilled chicken, ham or bacon.

Serves 4

INGREDIENTS

*400g/14oz can crushed pineapple in
  natural juice*
*30ml/2 tbsp light muscovado
  (brown) sugar*
30ml/2 tbsp wine vinegar
1 garlic clove, finely chopped
4 spring onions (scallions), finely chopped
2 red chillies, seeded and chopped
10 fresh basil leaves, finely shredded
salt and ground black pepper

1 Drain the pineapple and reserve 60ml/4 tbsp of the juice.

2 Place the juice in a small pan with the sugar and vinegar, then heat gently, stirring frequently, until the sugar dissolves. Remove the pan from the heat and season with salt and pepper to taste.

3 Place the pineapple, garlic, spring onions and chillies in a bowl and stir in the juice. Allow to cool for 5 minutes, then stir in the basil and serve.

VARIATION

This relish tastes extra special when made with fresh pineapple.

Papaya and Lemon Relish

THIS CHUNKY RELISH IS best made with a firm, unripe papaya. Leave for a week before eating to allow all the flavours to mellow. Store unopened jars in a cool place, away from sunlight. Serve with roast meats or with a robust cheese and crackers.

Makes about 450g/1lb

INGREDIENTS

1 large unripe papaya
1 onion, thinly sliced
40g/1½oz/⅓ cup raisins
250ml/8fl oz/1 cup red wine vinegar
juice of 2 lemons
150ml/¼ pint/⅔ cup elderflower cordial
150g/5oz/¾ cup golden granulated sugar
1 cinnamon stick
1 fresh bay leaf
2.5ml/½ tsp hot paprika
2.5ml/½ tsp salt

1 Peel the papaya and cut lengthways in half. Remove the seeds with a teaspoon. Use a sharp knife to cut the flesh into small chunks and place them in a pan. Add the onion slices and raisins, then stir in the red wine vinegar.

2 Bring the liquid to the boil, then immediately lower the heat and simmer for 10 minutes.

COOK'S TIP

The seeds of papaya are often discarded when the ripe fruit is used, but they have a peppery taste and make a delicious addition to a salad dressing.

3 Add all the remaining ingredients to the pan and bring to the boil, stirring constantly. Check that all the sugar has dissolved, then lower the heat and simmer for 50–60 minutes, or until the relish is thick and syrupy.

4 Remove and discard the bay leaf. Ladle the relish into hot, sterilized jars. Seal and label, and store in a cool, dark place for 1 week before using. Keep the relish chilled after opening.

Spicy Sweetcorn Relish

SERVE THIS SIMPLE SPICY relish with Red Onion Raita, Sweet Mango Relish and a plateful of crisp onion bhajis for a fabulous Indian-style appetizer.

Serves 4

INGREDIENTS

30ml/2 tbsp vegetable oil
1 large onion, chopped
1 red chilli, seeded and chopped
2 garlic cloves, chopped
5ml/1 tsp black mustard seeds
10ml/2 tsp hot curry powder
320g/11¼oz can sweetcorn, drained
grated rind and juice of 1 lime
45ml/3 tbsp chopped fresh coriander (cilantro)
salt and ground black pepper

1 Heat the oil in a large frying pan and cook the onion, chilli and garlic over a high heat for 5 minutes, until the onions are just beginning to brown.

COOK'S TIP

Use frozen rather than canned sweetcorn as the kernels are plump and moist.

2 Stir in the mustard seeds and curry powder, then cook for 2 minutes more, stirring, until the seeds start to splutter and the onions are browned.

3 Remove the fried onion and spice mixture from the heat and allow to cool completely. Transfer the mixture to a glass bowl.

4 Add the drained sweetcorn to the bowl containing the onion mixture and stir to mix.

5 Add the lime rind and juice, coriander and seasoning. Mix well, then cover and serve at room temperature.

Sweet Mango Relish

STIR A SPOONFUL OF this relish into
soups and stews for added flavour
or serve it with a wedge of Cheddar
cheese and chunks of crusty bread.

Makes 750ml/1¼ pints/3 cups

INGREDIENTS

2 large mangoes
1 cooking apple, peeled and chopped
2 shallots, chopped
4cm/1½ in piece fresh root ginger, chopped
2 garlic cloves, crushed
115g/4oz/⅔ cup small sultanas
   (golden raisins)
2 star anise
5ml/1 tsp ground cinnamon
2.5ml/½ tsp dried chilli flakes
2.5ml/½ tsp salt
175ml/6fl oz/¾ cup cider vinegar
130g/4½ oz/generous ½ cup light
   muscovado (brown) sugar

1 One at a time, hold the mangoes
upright on a chopping board and
use a large knife to slice the flesh away
from each side of the large stone (pit).

2 Using a smaller knife, carefully trim
away any flesh still clinging to the
top and bottom of the stone.

3 Score the flesh of the mango
halves deeply, taking care to avoid
cutting through the skin: make parallel
incisions about 1cm/½ in apart, then
turn and cut parallel lines in the
opposite direction.

4 Carefully turn the skin inside out so
that the mango flesh stands out like
small spikes. Slice the dice away from
the skin.

5 Place the diced mango, chopped
apple, shallots, ginger, garlic and
sultanas in a large, heavy pan. Add the
star anise, cinnamon, chilli, salt, vinegar
and sugar.

6 Bring to the boil, stirring constantly,
until the sugar has dissolved.
Reduce the heat and simmer very
gently for a further 4 minutes, stirring
occasionally, until the relish has reduced
and thickened.

7 Allow the relish to cool for about
5 minutes, then ladle it into warm,
sterilized jars. Cool completely, cover
and label. The relish may be stored in
the refrigerator for up to 2 months.
Keep the relish chilled after opening.

VARIATION

*Select alternative spices according to your
own taste: for example, you can add
juniper berries or cumin seeds in place
of the star anise.*

Chilli Relish

THIS SPICY RELISH will keep for at least a week in the refrigerator. Serve it with grilled sausages.

Serves 8

INGREDIENTS

6 tomatoes
30ml/2 tbsp olive oil
1 onion, roughly chopped
1 red (bell) pepper, seeded and chopped
2 garlic cloves, chopped
5ml/1 tsp ground cinnamon
5ml/1 tsp chilli flakes
5ml/1 tsp ground ginger
5ml/1 tsp salt
2.5ml/½ tsp ground black pepper
75g/3oz/6 tbsp light muscovado
 (brown) sugar
75ml/5 tbsp cider vinegar
handful of fresh basil leaves, chopped

1 Skewer each of the tomatoes in turn on a metal fork and hold in a gas flame for 1–2 minutes, turning, until the skin splits and wrinkles.

2 Slip off the tomato skins, then roughly chop the flesh.

3 Heat the olive oil in a pan. Add the chopped onion, red pepper and garlic to the pan.

4 Cook gently for 5–8 minutes, or until the pepper is softened. Add the chopped tomatoes, cover and cook for 5 minutes, until the tomatoes release their juices.

5 Stir in the cinnamon, chilli flakes, ginger, salt, pepper, sugar and vinegar. Bring gently to the boil, stirring, until the sugar dissolves.

6 Simmer, uncovered, for 20 minutes, or until the mixture is pulpy. Stir in the basil leaves and check the seasoning.

7 Allow to cool completely, then transfer to a glass jar or a plastic container with a tightly fitting lid. Store, covered, in the refrigerator.

COOK'S TIP

This relish thickens slightly on cooling, so do not worry if the mixture seems a little wet at the end of step 6.

VARIATION

Replace the fresh garlic with smoked garlic for a really smoky, barbecue flavour.

Bloody Mary Relish

SERVE THIS PERFECT PARTY relish with
sticks of crunchy cucumber or, on a
really special occasion, with freshly
shucked oysters.

Serves 2

INGREDIENTS

4 ripe tomatoes

1 celery stick

1 garlic clove

2 spring onions (scallions)

45ml/3 tbsp tomato juice

Worcestershire sauce, to taste

red Tabasco sauce, to taste

10ml/2 tsp horseradish sauce

15ml/1 tbsp vodka

juice of 1 lemon

salt and ground black pepper

1 Halve the tomatoes, celery and
garlic. Trim the spring onions.

2 Process the vegetables in a food
processor or blender until very
finely chopped. Transfer to a bowl.

3 Stir in the tomato juice and add a
few drops of Worcestershire sauce
and Tabasco to taste.

4 Stir in the horseradish sauce, vodka
and lemon juice. Season with salt
and ground black pepper, to taste.

VARIATION

*In the food processor or blender, add
1–2 fresh, seeded, red chillies with the
tomatoes, celery and garlic instead of
adding Tabasco sauce.*

Tart Tomato Relish

THE WHOLE LIME used in this recipe adds a pleasantly sour aftertaste. This is delicious served with grilled or roast pork or lamb.

Serves 4

INGREDIENTS

1 lime
450g/1lb cherry tomatoes
115g/4oz/½ cup dark muscovado (molasses) sugar
105ml/7 tbsp white wine vinegar
5ml/1 tsp salt
2 pieces stem (crystallized) ginger, chopped

1 Slice the whole lime thinly, then chop it into small pieces; do not remove the rind.

VARIATION

If preferred, use ordinary tomatoes, roughly chopped, in place of the cherry tomatoes used here.

2 Place the whole tomatoes, sugar, vinegar, salt, ginger and lime together in a pan.

3 Bring to the boil, stirring until the sugar dissolves, then simmer rapidly for 45 minutes. Stir regularly until the liquid has evaporated and the relish is thickened and pulpy.

4 Allow the relish to cool for about 5 minutes, then spoon it into clean jars. Cool completely, cover and store in the refrigerator for up to 1 month.

Toffee Onion Relish

Slow, gentle cooking reduces the onions to a soft, caramelized golden brown relish in this recipe. This relish adds a sweet flavour to a strong-flavoured cheese or makes an ideal accompaniment to flans and quiches.

Serves 4

INGREDIENTS

3 large onions
50g/2oz/¼ cup butter
30ml/2 tbsp olive oil
30ml/2 tbsp light muscovado
  (brown) sugar
30ml/2 tbsp pickled capers
30ml/2 tbsp chopped fresh parsley
salt and ground black pepper

1 Peel the onions and cut them in half vertically through the core, then slice them thinly.

2 Heat the butter and oil together in a large, heavy pan. Add the sliced onions and sugar, and cook very gently for about 30 minutes over a low heat, stirring occasionally, until the onions are reduced to a soft rich-brown, toffee-like mixture.

3 Roughly chop the capers and stir into the browned onion mixture. Allow to cool completely and transfer to a bowl.

COOK'S TIP

Choose a heavy pan to cook the relish in, to get an evenly browned toffee mixture without the risk of burning.

4 Stir in the chopped parsley and add salt and freshly ground black pepper to taste. Cover and chill until ready to serve.

VARIATION

Try making this recipe with red onions or shallots for a subtle variation in flavour.

Red Onion Marmalade

THIS IS A RICH and delicious marmalade, and makes a particularly good accompaniment to barbecued or grilled salmon.

Serves 4

INGREDIENTS

5 red onions
50g/2oz/¼ cup butter
175ml/6fl oz/¾ cup red wine vinegar
50ml/2fl oz/¼ cup crème de cassis
50ml/2fl oz/¼ cup grenadine
50ml/2fl oz/¼ cup red wine
salt and ground black pepper

1 Remove the skins from the red onions, discard, then slice the onions.

2 Melt the butter in a large, heavy pan and add the sliced onions. Sauté the onions for 5 minutes, or until golden brown.

3 Stir in the wine vinegar, crème de cassis, grenadine and wine and continue to cook for about 10 minutes, or until the liquid has almost entirely evaporated and the onions are glazed. Season well with salt and freshly ground black pepper.

COOK'S TIP

If serving this marmalade with barbecued (grilled) salmon, try to find pieces that are at least 2.5cm/1in thick. Brush them with olive oil, season with salt and ground black pepper, and cook on a medium barbecue for about 6–8 minutes, turning once during cooking.

Apple and Red Onion Marmalade

THIS MARMALADE CHUTNEY is good enough to eat on its own. Serve it with good quality pork sausages for thoroughly modern hot dogs, or in a ham sandwich instead of mustard.

Makes about 450g/1lb

INGREDIENTS

60ml/4 tbsp extra virgin olive oil
900g/2lb red onions, thinly sliced
75g/3oz/6 tbsp demerara (raw) sugar
2 eating apples
90ml/6 tbsp cider vinegar

1 Heat the oil in a large, heavy pan and add the onions.

2 Stir in the sugar and cook, uncovered, over a medium heat for about 40 minutes, stirring occasionally, or until the onions have softened.

3 Peel, core and grate the apples. Add them to the pan with the vinegar and continue to cook for 20 minutes, or until the chutney is thick and sticky. Spoon into sterilized jars and cover.

4 When cool, label and store in the refrigerator for up to 1 month.

VARIATION

If you like, add a cinnamon stick to the pan during cooking to impart a mild, sweet spice flavour. Remove the spice before bottling the marmalade chutney in sterilized jars.

Old-fashioned Pickle

THIS SIMPLE, OLD-FASHIONED pickle is quite delicious with cold meats or cheese, with a hunk of fresh crusty bread and butter on the side.

Makes about 1.3–1.6kg/3–3¹/₂lb

INGREDIENTS

900g/2lb cucumbers, scrubbed and cut in
*   5mm/¹/₄in slices*
4 onions, very thinly sliced
30ml/2 tbsp salt
350ml/12fl oz/1¹/₂ cups cider vinegar
300g/11 oz/generous 1¹/₂ cups sugar
30ml/2 tbsp mustard seeds
30ml/2 tbsp celery seeds
1.5ml/¹/₄ tsp ground turmeric
1.5ml/¹/₄ tsp cayenne pepper

COOK'S TIP

Avoid using metal lids or seals, as these may react with the acid in the pickle.

1 Put the sliced cucumbers and onions in a large bowl and sprinkle with the salt. Mix well. Cover loosely and leave to stand for 3 hours.

2 Drain the vegetables. Rinse well under cold running water and then drain again.

3 Prepare some heatproof glass jars (such as preserving jars). Wash them well in warm soapy water and rinse thoroughly in clean warm water.

4 Place the jars on a baking sheet in the oven at 150°C/300°F/Gas 2 for 30 minutes to sterilize. Keep the jars hot until ready to use.

5 Combine the remaining ingredients in a large, non-reactive pan and bring to the boil. Add the drained cucumbers and onions. Reduce the heat and simmer for 2–3 minutes. Do not boil or the pickles will be limp.

6 Spoon the hot vegetables into the hot jars. Add enough of the liquid to come to 1cm/¹/₂in from the top. Carefully wipe the jars with a clean damp cloth.

7 To seal, cover the surface of the pickles with a waxed disc, waxed side down, then put on the jar lids. The pickles should be sealed immediately. If the lid does not have a ring gasket, first cover the top of the jar with a plastic wrap or cellophane cover, then screw the plastic top down tightly. Leave in a cool dark place for at least 4 weeks.

Christmas Chutney

THIS SAVOURY MIXTURE OF spices and dried fruit takes its inspiration from mincemeat, and makes a delicious addition to the festive buffet.

Makes about 1–1.6kg/2¼–3½lb

INGREDIENTS
450g/1lb cooking apples, peeled, cored
    and chopped
500g/1¼lb/3⅓ cups luxury mixed dried fruit
grated rind of 1 orange
30ml/2 tbsp mixed (apple pie) spice
150ml/¼ pint/⅔ cup cider vinegar
350g/12oz/1½ cups light muscovado
    (brown) sugar

Place the chopped apples, dried fruit and grated orange rind in a large, heavy pan. Stir in the mixed spice, vinegar and sugar. Heat the ingredients gently, stirring until all the sugar has dissolved.

2 Bring to the boil, then lower the heat and simmer the mixture for 40–45 minutes, stirring occasionally, until thick.

3 Ladle into warm, sterilized jars, cover and seal. Keep for 1 month before using.

COOK'S TIPS

• Watch the chutney carefully towards the end of the cooking time, as it has a tendency to catch on the base of the pan. Stir frequently at this stage.
• Store in the refrigerator after opening.

Fig and Date Chutney

THIS RECIPE IS USUALLY made with dried figs and dates, but fresh fruit provides a superb flavour and texture.

Makes about 450g/1lb

INGREDIENTS

1 orange

5 large fresh figs, coarsely chopped

350g/12oz/2½ cups fresh dates, peeled, stoned (pitted) and chopped

2 onions, chopped

5cm/2in piece of fresh root ginger, peeled and finely grated

5ml/1 tsp dried crushed chillies

300g/11oz/generous 1½ cups golden granulated sugar

300ml/½ pint/1¼ cups spiced preserving vinegar

2.5ml/½ tsp salt

COOK'S TIP

Figs are in season for only a short time, so buy when you see them.

1 Finely grate the rind of the orange, then cut off the remaining pith.

VARIATION

If you would rather use dried figs and dates to make the chutney, you will need to increase the amount of preserving vinegar to 450ml/¾ pint/scant 2 cups. Remove the stones (pits) from the dates and then coarsely chop both the figs and the dates.

2 Place the orange segments in a large, heavy pan with the chopped figs and dates. Add the rind, then stir in the remaining ingredients. Bring to the boil, stirring until the sugar has dissolved, then lower the heat and simmer gently for 1 hour or until thickened and pulpy, stirring frequently.

3 Spoon into hot sterilized jars. Seal while the chutney is still hot and label when cold. Store in a cool dark place for 1 week before using. Keep the jars in the refrigerator once they have been opened.

Fresh Pineapple and Mint Chutney

THIS REFRESHING, LIGHT FRUIT chutney has a fresh flavour; it is good with rich meat dishes, particularly lamb or pork.

Makes about 1kg/2¼lb

INGREDIENTS

250ml/8fl oz/1 cup raspberry vinegar
250ml/8fl oz/1 cup dry white wine
1 small pineapple, peeled and chopped
2 medium-size oranges, peeled
   and chopped
2 eating apples, peeled and chopped
1 red (bell) pepper, seeded and diced
1½ onions, finely chopped
60ml/4 tbsp honey
pinch of salt
1 whole clove
4 black peppercorns
30ml/2 tbsp chopped fresh mint

1 In a large pan, combine the raspberry vinegar and white wine, and bring to a boil. Boil for 3 minutes.

2 Add the remaining ingredients, except the mint, and stir to blend. Simmer gently for about 30 minutes, stirring occasionally.

3 Transfer to a strainer set over a bowl and drain, pressing down to extract the liquid. Remove and discard the clove and peppercorns. Set the fruit mixture aside.

4 Return the strained juice to the pan and boil until reduced by two-thirds. Pour over the fruit mixture.

5 Stir in the mint. Leave to stand for 6–8 hours before serving.

COOK'S TIP

The chutney will keep for about 1 week in the refrigerator. If you can get pineapple mint, this adds a delightful scent to the finished chutney.

Mango Chutney

THIS CLASSIC CHUTNEY IS frequently served with curries and Indian poppadums, but it is also delicious with baked ham or a traditional cheese and crusty bread lunch.

Makes about 450g/1lb

INGREDIENTS

3 firm green mangoes
150ml/¼ pint/⅔ cup cider vinegar
130g/4½ oz/generous ½ cup light
   muscovado (brown) sugar
1 small red finger chilli or jalapeño chilli, split
2.5cm/1 in piece of fresh root ginger, peeled
   and finely chopped
1 garlic clove, finely chopped
5 cardamom pods, bruised
2.5ml/½ tsp coriander seeds, crushed
1 bay leaf
2.5ml/½ tsp salt

1 Peel the mangoes and cut the flesh off the stone (pit). Slice them, then cut into small chunks or wedges.

COOK'S TIP

Green, under-ripe mangoes have a sharp, tangy flavour, quite unlike the fragrant sweetness of ripe ones, but ideal for relishes and chutneys to serve with savoury foods.

2 Place these in a large pan, add the vinegar and cover. Cook over a low heat for 10 minutes.

3 Stir in the sugar, chilli, ginger, garlic, bruised cardamom pods and coriander seeds. Add the bay leaf and salt. Bring to the boil slowly, stirring the mixture frequently.

4 Lower the heat and simmer, uncovered, for 30 minutes, or until the mixture is thick and syrupy. Remove the cardamom pods if you prefer and remove and discard the bay leaf.

5 Ladle into hot, sterilized jars. Leave to cool, then seal and label. Store in a cool, dark place for 1 week before eating. Keep chilled after opening.

Roasted Red Pepper and Chilli Jelly

THE HINT OF CHILLI in this glowing red jelly makes it ideal for spicing up hot or cold roast meat. The jelly is also good stirred into sauces.

Makes about 900g/2lb

INGREDIENTS
8 red (bell) peppers, quartered and seeded
4 fresh red chillies, halved and seeded
1 onion, roughly chopped
2 garlic cloves, roughly chopped
250ml/8fl oz/1 cup water
250ml/8fl oz/1 cup white wine vinegar
7.5ml/1½ tsp salt
450g/1lb/2¼ cups preserving sugar
13g/⅓ oz sachet powdered pectin (about 25ml/1½ tbsp)

COOK'S TIP

It is not essential to use preserving sugar, but it produces less scum.

1 Place the peppers, skin-side up, on a rack in a grill (broiler) pan. Grill (broil) until blistered and blackened. Place in a plastic bag until cool enough to handle, then remove the skins.

2 Purée the peppers with the chillies, onion, garlic and water in a food processor or blender. Press the purée through a nylon strainer set over a bowl, pressing hard with a wooden spoon, to extract as much juice as possible. There should be roughly 750ml/1¼ pints/3 cups.

3 Scrape the purée into a large, stainless steel pan. Add the vinegar and salt. In a bowl, mix the sugar and pectin, then stir into the liquid.

4 Heat gently until both the sugar and pectin have dissolved, then bring to a full rolling boil. Boil, stirring frequently, for exactly 4 minutes.

5 Remove the jelly from the heat and pour into warm, sterilized jars. Leave to cool and set, then cover. Keep opened jars in the refrigerator.

Dressings and Marinades

The primary function of dressings and marinades is to add or balance flavour, and this can make all the difference to even the simplest foods. Both are usually based on a mix of oil and an acidic ingredient, such as vinegar or fruit juice, with aromatic additions, such as herbs, garlic or spices for a more individual flavour.

Dressings are used to moisten foods, add variety and lift the flavour of any type of salad, from simple green leaves to substantial main meal salads. They are also of benefit to other foods, such as lightly cooked spears of asparagus, pak choi (bok choy), or crudités.

Marinades are used not only to add flavour to foods, but also to tenderize meats or add moisture to dry foods, either before cooking or as a baste during cooking. A light summer herb marinade makes the world of difference to the flavour of a simple piece of fish or meat, or try a peppered citrus marinade to add a delicious zing to meaty-textured monkfish. The tenderizing effect, caused by the acid content in marinades, is particularly beneficial for tough meats or poultry. A yogurt marinade has a tenderizing effect, too, with the added benefit of forming a deliciously tangy crust on the outside of grilled (broiled) food.

Avocado Dressing with Crudités

THIS CREAMY-TEXTURED DRESSING is actually quite light, and also makes a good dressing for tomato salads.

Makes about 450ml/¾ pint/ scant 2 cups

INGREDIENTS

30ml/2 tbsp wine vinegar
2.5ml/½ tsp salt, or to taste
4ml/¾ tsp ground white pepper
½ red onion, coarsely chopped
45ml/3 tbsp olive oil
1 large ripe avocado, halved and
　stoned (pitted)
15ml/1 tbsp fresh lemon juice
45ml/3 tbsp natural (plain) yogurt
45ml/3 tbsp water, or as needed
30ml/2 tbsp chopped fresh
　coriander (cilantro)
raw or briefly cooked cold vegetables,
　to serve

1 In a bowl, combine the vinegar and salt and stir with a fork to dissolve. Stir in the ground white pepper, chopped red onion and olive oil.

2 Scoop the avocado flesh into a food processor or blender with a teaspoon. Add the lemon juice and onion dressing and process just enough to blend.

3 Add the yogurt and water and process until the mixture is smooth. If desired, add more water to thin. Taste and adjust the seasoning according to taste.

4 Spoon the mixture into a bowl. Stir in the coriander. Serve immediately with the raw or briefly cooked cold vegetables.

COOK'S TIP

This versatile dressing need not be limited to serving with crudités and salads. Serve it as a sauce with grilled (broiled) chicken or fish, or use it on sandwiches in place of mayonnaise or mustard, or to provide a cool contrast to any sort of spicy food.

Lime Dressing with Pak Choi

FOR THIS THAI RECIPE, the lime dressing is traditionally made using fish sauce, but vegetarians could use mushroom ketchup instead. Beware, this is a fiery dish!

Serves 4

INGREDIENTS
6 spring onions (scallions)
2 pak choi (bok choy)
30ml/2 tbsp oil
3 fresh red chillies, cut into thin strips
4 garlic cloves, thinly sliced
15ml/1 tbsp crushed peanuts
salt

For the lime dressing
15–30ml/1–2 tbsp fish sauce
30ml/2 tbsp lime juice
250ml/8fl oz/1 cup coconut milk

COOK'S TIP

Coconut milk is available in cans. Alternatively, creamed coconut (coconut cream) is available in packets. Place about 115g/4oz in a jug (pitcher) and pour over 250ml/8fl oz/1 cup boiling water. Stir until dissolved.

1 To make the dressing, blend together the fish sauce and lime juice, and then stir in the coconut milk.

2 Slice the spring onions diagonally, including all but the tips of the green parts. Keep the white parts separate from the green.

3 Cut the pak choi into very fine shreds.

4 Heat the oil in a wok and stir-fry the chillies for 2–3 minutes, or until crisp. Transfer to a plate using a slotted spoon. Stir-fry the garlic for 30–60 seconds, or until golden brown, and transfer to the plate with the chillies.

5 Stir-fry the white parts of the spring onions for 2–3 minutes and then add the green parts and stir-fry for 1 minute. Add to the plate with the chillies and garlic.

6 Bring a large pan of salted water to the boil and add the shredded pak choi. Stir twice and then drain immediately.

7 Place the warmed pak choi in a large bowl, add the dressing and stir well.

8 Spoon into a large serving bowl and sprinkle with the crushed peanuts and the stir-fried chilli mixture. Serve either warm or cold, as an accompaniment to rice dishes.

Creamy Raspberry Dressing with Asparagus

RASPBERRY VINEGAR gives this quick dressing a refreshing, tangy fruit flavour – an ideal accompaniment to asparagus.

Serves 4

INGREDIENTS

675g/1½ lb thin asparagus spears
115g/4oz/1½ cups fresh raspberries,
to garnish

For the creamy raspberry dressing
30ml/2 tbsp raspberry vinegar
2.5ml/½ tsp salt
5ml/1 tsp Dijon-style mustard
60ml/4 tbsp crème fraîche or natural
(plain) yogurt
ground white pepper

1 Fill a pan with water to a depth of about 10cm/4in and bring to the boil. Trim the tough ends of the asparagus spears.

COOK'S TIP

Cook the asparagus and make the sauce in advance, then chill in the refrigerator until needed. Serve cold.

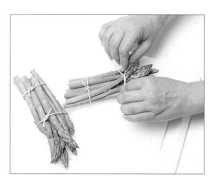

2 Tie the asparagus spears into two bundles. Lower the bundles into the boiling water and cook for 3–5 minutes, or until just tender.

3 Remove the asparagus and immerse it in cold water to stop the cooking. Drain and untie the bundles. Pat dry. Chill for 1 hour.

4 To make the dressing, mix the vinegar and salt in a bowl and stir with a fork until dissolved. Stir in the mustard, crème fraîche or yogurt. Add pepper to taste. Place the asparagus on plates and drizzle the dressing across the middle of the spears. Garnish with fresh raspberries.

Coriander Dressing with Chicken Salad

SERVE THIS SALAD WARM to make the most of the wonderful flavour of barbecued or grilled chicken basted with a marinade of coriander, sesame and mustard, and finished with a matching dressing.

Serves 6

INGREDIENTS

*4 medium skinless, boneless
  chicken breast portions*
225g/8oz mangetouts (snow peas)
*2 heads decorative lettuce such as lollo
  rosso or oakleaf*
3 carrots, cut into batons
*175g/6oz/2¼ cups button (white)
  mushrooms, sliced*
6 bacon rashers (strips), fried and chopped
*15ml/1 tbsp chopped fresh coriander
  (cilantro), to garnish*

For the coriander dressing
120ml/4fl oz/½ cup lemon juice
30ml/2 tbsp wholegrain mustard
250ml/8fl oz/1 cup olive oil
75ml/5 tbsp sesame oil
5ml/1 tsp coriander seeds, crushed

1 Mix all the dressing ingredients in a bowl. Place the chicken portions in a dish and pour over half the dressing. Marinate overnight in the refrigerator. Chill the remaining dressing.

2 Cook the mangetouts for about 2 minutes in boiling water, then refresh in cold water.

3 Tear the lettuces into small pieces and mix with all the other salad ingredients and the bacon. Arrange in individual bowls.

4 Cook the chicken portions on a medium barbecue or under a grill (broiler) for 10–15 minutes, basting with the marinade and turning once, until cooked through.

COOK'S TIP

If you have any spare dressing left over, store it in a screw-topped jar in the refrigerator for up to 4 days. Use the dressing for drizzling over other salads.

5 Slice the chicken on the diagonal into thin pieces. Divide among the bowls of salad and add some of the dressing to each dish. Combine quickly and sprinkle some fresh coriander over each bowl.

Ginger and Lime Marinade

THIS FRAGRANT MARINADE will guarantee a mouthwatering aroma from the barbecue, and is perfect with shellfish.

Serves 4

INGREDIENTS
*225g/8oz peeled raw tiger prawns
   (jumbo shrimp)*
¹/₃ cucumber
15ml/1 tbsp sunflower oil
15ml/1 tbsp sesame seed oil
175g/6oz mangetouts (snow peas)
4 spring onions (scallions), diagonally sliced
*30ml/2 tbsp chopped fresh coriander
   (cilantro), to garnish*

For the ginger and lime marinade
15ml/1 tbsp clear honey
15ml/1 tbsp light soy sauce
15ml/1 tbsp dry sherry
2 garlic cloves, crushed
*small piece of fresh root ginger, peeled and
   finely chopped*
juice of 1 lime

1 Mix together the marinade ingredients, add the prawns and leave to marinate for 1–2 hours.

2 Prepare the cucumber. Slice it in half lengthways, scoop out the seeds, then slice each half neatly into crescents. Set aside.

3 Heat both oils in a large frying pan or wok. Drain the prawns, reserving the marinade, and stir-fry over a high heat for 4 minutes, or until they begin to turn pink. Add the mangetouts and cucumber and stir-fry for 2 minutes.

4 Stir in the reserved marinade, heat through, then stir in the spring onions and sprinkle with chopped fresh coriander to garnish.

VARIATION

This marinade is also a good one to use with larger pieces of fish for grilling (broiling), such as salmon, trout or tuna, and is as delicious with chicken or pork as it is with prawns.

Peppered Citrus Marinade for Monkfish

MONKFISH IS A FIRM, meaty fish that cooks well on the barbecue. Serve with a green salad.

Serves 4

INGREDIENTS

2 monkfish tails, about 350g/12oz each
1 lime
1 lemon
2 oranges
handful of fresh thyme sprigs
30ml/2 tbsp olive oil
15ml/1 tbsp mixed peppercorns,
    roughly crushed
salt and ground black pepper

1 Using a sharp kitchen knife, remove any skin from the monkfish tails. Cut the fish carefully down one side of the backbone, sliding the knife between the bone and flesh, to remove the fillet on one side.

2 Turn the fish and repeat on the other side, to remove the second fillet. Repeat on the second tail. Place the 4 fillets flat on a chopping board.

3 Cut 2 slices from each of the citrus fruits and arrange them over 2 of the fillets.

4 Add a few sprigs of fresh thyme, and sprinkle with plenty of salt and ground black pepper. Finely grate the rind from the remaining fruit and sprinkle it over the fish.

5 Lay the other 2 fillets on top and tie them firmly at intervals.

6 Squeeze the juice from the citrus fruits and mix it with the olive oil and seasoning. Spoon over the fish. Cover with clear film (plastic wrap) and marinate in the refrigerator for about 1 hour, turning the fish occasionally and spooning the marinade over it.

7 Drain the fish, reserving the marinade, and sprinkle with the crushed peppercorns. Grill (broil) for 15–20 minutes, basting frequently with the marinade.

VARIATION

If you prefer, remove the peel from the fruit before placing between the fillets.

Orange and Green Peppercorn Marinade for Sea Bass

THIS IS AN EXCELLENT light marinade for using with whole fish. The cooked fish, in the lovely soft-coloured marinade, needs only a fresh herb sprig as garnish. Other suitable fish for this recipe are sea trout or sea bream.

Serves 4

INGREDIENTS
1 medium whole sea bass, cleaned

For the peppercorn marinade
1 red onion
2 small oranges
90ml/6 tbsp light olive oil
30ml/2 tbsp cider vinegar
30ml/2 tbsp green peppercorns in brine, drained
30ml/2 tbsp chopped fresh parsley
salt and sugar, to taste

1 With a sharp knife, slash the sea bass 3–4 times on both sides.

2 Line an ovenproof dish with foil. Peel and slice the onion and oranges. Place half in the base of the dish, place the fish on top, and cover with the remaining onion and orange.

3 Mix the remaining marinade ingredients and pour over the fish. Cover and stand for 4 hours, occasionally spooning the marinade over the top.

4 Preheat the oven to 180°C/350°F/ Gas 4. Fold the foil over the fish and seal loosely. Bake for 15 minutes per 450g/1lb, plus 15 minutes over. Serve with the juices.

Summer Herb Marinade for Salmon

MAKE THE BEST USE of summer herbs in this marinade, which can also be used with veal, chicken, pork or lamb.

Serves 4

INGREDIENTS

4 salmon steaks or fillets, about 175g/6oz each

For the herb marinade

large handful of fresh herb sprigs, e.g. chervil, thyme, parsley, sage, chives, rosemary, oregano
90ml/6 tbsp olive oil
45ml/3 tbsp tarragon vinegar
1 garlic clove, crushed
2 spring onions (scallions), chopped
salt and ground black pepper

1 Discard any coarse stalks or damaged leaves from the herbs, then chop them very finely.

2 Add the chopped herbs to the remaining marinade ingredients in a large bowl. Stir to mix thoroughly.

3 Place the salmon in the bowl and spoon the marinade over. Cover and leave to marinate in a cool place for 4–6 hours.

4 Drain the fish when you are ready to cook it on the barbecue. Use the marinade to baste the fish occasionally during cooking.

COOK'S TIP

Keep the discarded herb stalks to throw on to the barbecue coals when you cook, to add an extra dimension to the flavour.

Spicy Yogurt Marinade for Chicken

PLAN THIS DISH WELL in advance; the extra-long marinating time is necessary to develop a really mellow spicy flavour.

Serves 6

INGREDIENTS
6 chicken pieces
juice of I lemon
5ml/I tsp salt
fresh mint, lemon and lime, to garnish

For the yogurt marinade
5ml/I tsp coriander seeds
10ml/2 tsp cumin seeds
6 cloves
2 bay leaves
I onion, quartered
2 garlic cloves
5cm/2in piece fresh root ginger, peeled and roughly chopped
2.5ml/½ tsp chilli powder
5ml/I tsp ground turmeric
150ml/¼ pint/⅔ cup natural (plain) yogurt

1 Skin the chicken pieces and make deep slashes in the fleshiest parts with a sharp knife. Sprinkle the lemon juice and salt over, and rub in.

2 Make the marinade. Spread the coriander and cumin seeds, cloves and bay leaves in the base of a large frying pan and dry-fry over a moderate heat until the bay leaves are crispy.

3 Allow the spice mixture to cool, then grind it coarsely in a mortar with a pestle.

4 Finely mince (grind) the onion, garlic and ginger in a food processor or blender with the ground spices, chilli, turmeric and yogurt. Strain in the lemon juice from the chicken.

5 Arrange the chicken in a single layer in a roasting pan. Pour the marinade over, then cover and chill for 24–36 hours, turning the chicken pieces occasionally.

6 Preheat the oven to 200°C/400°F/ Gas 6. Cook the chicken for 45 minutes, or until the juices run clear when the meat is pierced. Serve hot or cold, garnished with fresh mint and slices of lemon or lime.

VARIATION

This marinade will also work well brushed over skewers of lamb or pork fillet prior to cooking on a barbecue or under the grill (broiler).

Lavender Balsamic Marinade for Lamb

LAVENDER IS AN UNUSUAL flavour to use with meat, but its heady, summery scent works well with chargrilled lamb. Use the flower heads as garnish.

Serves 4

INGREDIENTS
4 racks of lamb, with 3–4 cutlets each

For the balsamic marinade
1 shallot, finely chopped
45ml/3 tbsp chopped fresh lavender
15ml/1 tbsp balsamic vinegar
30ml/2 tbsp olive oil
15ml/1 tbsp lemon juice
handful of lavender sprigs
salt and ground black pepper

1 Place the racks of lamb in a large mixing bowl or wide dish and sprinkle the chopped shallot over.

2 Sprinkle the chopped fresh lavender over the lamb in the bowl.

3 Beat together the vinegar, olive oil and lemon juice and pour them over the lamb. Season well with salt and ground black pepper and then turn the meat to coat evenly.

4 Sprinkle a few lavender sprigs under the grill (broiler) or on the coals of a medium-hot barbecue. Cook the lamb for 15–20 minutes, turning once and basting with any remaining marinade, until golden brown on the outside and still slightly pink in the centre. Just before serving, garnish with lavender flower heads.

Red Wine and Juniper Marinade for Lamb

JUNIPER BERRIES HAVE A pungent flavour which is ideal to flavour lamb.

Serves 4–6

INGREDIENTS

675g/1½lb boned leg of lamb, cubed
2 carrots, cut into batons
225g/8oz baby (pearl) onions or shallots
115g/4oz/1½ cups button
  (white) mushrooms
30ml/2 tbsp vegetable oil
150ml/¼ pint/⅔ cup stock
30ml/2 tbsp beurre manié
salt and ground black pepper

For the red wine and juniper marinade
4 rosemary sprigs
8 dried juniper berries, lightly crushed
8 black peppercorns, lightly crushed
300ml/½ pint/1¼ cups red wine

1 Place the meat in a bowl, add the vegetables, rosemary, juniper berries and peppercorns, then pour over the wine. Cover and leave in a cool place for 4–5 hours, stirring once or twice during this time.

2 Remove the lamb and vegetables with a slotted spoon and set aside. Strain the marinade into a jug (pitcher).

3 Preheat the oven to 160°C/325°F/ Gas 3. Heat the oil in a pan and fry the meat and vegetables in batches until lightly browned. Transfer to a casserole and pour over the reserved marinade and stock. Cover and cook in the oven for 2 hours.

4 About 20 minutes before the end of cooking, stir in the beurre manié, then cover and return to the oven. Season to taste before serving.

COOK'S TIP

Beurre manié is made of equal parts of butter and flour blended together. It is used as a thickening agent and should be added a small piece at a time.

Lemon and Rosemary Marinade for Lamb

MARINATE THE leg of lamb overnight in the refrigerator so that the flavours have plenty of time to penetrate the meat fully.

Serves 6

INGREDIENTS

1.3–1.6kg/3–3½lb leg of lamb
2 garlic cloves, sliced
15ml/1 tbsp cornflour (cornstarch)

For the lemon and rosemary marinade

1 lemon, sliced
6 fresh rosemary sprigs
4 fresh lemon thyme sprigs
300ml/½ pint/1¼ cups dry white wine
60ml/4 tbsp olive oil
salt and ground black pepper

1 Make small cuts over the lamb surface. Insert a garlic piece in each.

2 Place the lamb in a roasting pan, with the lemon slices and herbs arranged over it.

3 Mix the wine, oil and seasoning and pour over the lamb. Cover and leave in a cool place for 4–6 hours, turning occasionally.

4 Preheat the oven to 180°C/350°F/ Gas 4. Roast the lamb for 25 minutes per 450g/1lb plus another 25 minutes. Baste with the marinade.

VARIATION

You can also use lemon and rosemary marinade for chicken pieces, but you must roast the meat without the marinade or it will become tough. Use the marinade for making into gravy when the chicken is cooked.

5 When the lamb is cooked, transfer to a warmed plate to rest. Drain the excess fat from the pan. Blend the cornflour with a little cold water and stir into the juices. Stir over a moderate heat for 2–3 minutes, then adjust the seasoning.

Chinese Sesame Marinade for Beef Strips

1 To make the marinade, blend the cornflour with the rice wine or sherry. Add the other marinade ingredients. Trim the steak and cut into thin strips about 1 x 5cm/½ x 2in. Stir into the marinade, cover and leave in a cool place for 3–4 hours.

2 Place the sesame seeds in a large frying pan or wok. Dry-fry over a moderate heat, shaking the pan until the seeds are golden. Set aside.

3 Heat the oils in the frying pan. Drain the beef, reserving the marinade, and brown a few pieces at a time. Remove with a slotted spoon.

4 Add the mushrooms and pepper and fry for 2–3 minutes, stirring. Add the spring onions and cook for 1 minute.

5 Add the beef and reserved marinade, and stir over a moderate heat for 2 minutes, or until evenly coated with the glaze. Sprinkle with the toasted sesame seeds, and serve.

TOASTED SESAME SEEDS BRING their distinctive smoky aroma to this Chinese marinade.

Serves 4

INGREDIENTS
450g/1lb rump (round) steak
30ml/2 tbsp sesame seeds
15ml/1 tbsp sesame oil
30ml/2 tbsp vegetable oil
115g/4oz/1½ cups small
   mushrooms, quartered
1 green (bell) pepper, seeded and diced
4 spring onions (scallions), chopped diagonally

For the Chinese sesame marinade
10ml/2 tsp cornflour (cornstarch)
30ml/2 tbsp rice wine or sherry
15ml/1 tbsp lemon juice
15ml/1 tbsp soy sauce
few drops Tabasco sauce
2.5cm/1in piece fresh root ginger, peeled
   and grated
1 garlic clove, crushed

VARIATION

This marinade would also be good with lean pork fillet or chicken breast portions.

Winter-spiced Ale Marinade for Beef

THIS MARINADE can also be used in a casserole of beef or lamb pieces.

Serves 6

INGREDIENTS

1.3kg/3lb topside (pot roast) rump
   (round) steak

For the winter-spiced ale marinade

1 onion, sliced

2 carrots, sliced

2 celery sticks, sliced

2–3 parsley stalks, lightly crushed

large fresh thyme sprig

2 bay leaves

6 cloves, lightly crushed

1 cinnamon stick

8 black peppercorns

300ml/½ pint/1¼ cups brown ale
   (dark beer)

45ml/3 tbsp vegetable oil

30ml/2 tbsp beurre manié

salt and ground black pepper

1 Put the meat in a plastic bag placed inside a large, deep bowl. Add the vegetables, herbs and spices, then pour the ale over. Seal the bag and leave in a cool place for 5–6 hours.

2 Remove the beef and set aside. Strain the marinade into a bowl, reserving the marinade.

3 Heat the oil in a flameproof casserole. Fry the vegetables until lightly browned, then remove with a slotted spoon and set aside. Brown the beef all over in the remaining oil.

4 Preheat the oven to 160°C/325°F/ Gas 3.

5 Return the vegetables to the casserole and pour the reserved marinade over the beef.

6 Cover the casserole and cook in the oven for 2½ hours. Turn the beef 2–3 times in the marinade during cooking.

7 To serve, remove the beef and slice neatly. Arrange on a plate with the vegetables. Gradually stir the beurre manié into the marinade and cook until thickened. Adjust the seasoning.

COOK'S TIP

A rich, dark brown ale has the ideal flavour for this recipe, but the choice depends on your own taste.

Index